THE
AMATEUR
ASTRONOMER
Explorations and Investigations
by Fred Schaaf

An Amateur Science Series Book
FRANKLIN WATTS
New York · Chicago · London · Toronto · Sydney

Illustrations by Lloyd Birmingham
Photographs copyright ©: University of California Regents, UCO/Lick Observatory:
pp. 10, 56, 137, 141; Ray Maher: p. 23; Fred Schaaf/Tom Connelly: p. 74;
Edmund Scientific Co./Charles Capen: p. 103.

Library of Congress Cataloging-in-Publication Data

Schaaf, Fred.
The amateur astronomer : explorations and investigations / by Fred Schaaf.
p.   cm.—(An Amateur science series book)
Includes bibliographical references and index.
ISBN 0-531-11138-5
1. Astronomy—Amateurs' manuals.   2. Astronomy—Observers'
manuals.   I. Title.   II. Series.
QB63.S39   1994
520—dc2093-31788 CIP AC

Contents

One Evening's Adventure

Most people think the idea of a vacation to faraway and strange places sounds exciting. Of course, they want to be sure that a vacation like that won't take too much time or money (which it usually does), and they don't want to have to put up with anything uncomfortable or inconvenient (which they usually do).

Imagine vacations to the most distant and strange—but dazzlingly beautiful—places possible. Now imagine that taking these trips costs you so little (usually no money at all) and is so quick and easy that you can take them many nights each month with no more inconvenience than a little coldness or sleepiness if you're not careful.

Does all this sound too good to be true? Well, it is true, for the journeys to adventure I'm talking about are the ones you can have, perhaps even from your own yard or window, when you become an amateur astronomer.

Astronomy is the study of everything in outer space—including our Earth itself when we consider it as one planet among many. Astronomers deal with what is in one way the biggest of all topics: the universe. The universe can be defined as the sum total of everything in outer space (including outer space itself) that we can detect, or think might be detectable. Astronomers concern themselves with planets millions of miles away, with galaxies whose light takes millions of years to reach us. But here's the most amazing fact of all: you can see some of those planets right out your window, look with your unaided eyes at one of those galaxies glowing right overhead on an autumn evening.

Looking at such sights—not just reading about them but going out to see them for yourself—is what amateur astronomy is all about. This is one science in which many of the great objects of interest can be seen from where you live, wherever you may live. It is a science in which amateurs working from their own backyards can sometimes help professionals discover comets and exploding stars. Astronomy is also a field of study that can give you not just larger physical perspectives but larger mental perspectives—a bigger, richer view—on everything in life. When astronauts started going into space they saw for themselves what a precious, fragile, and somehow even small thing the Earth is—but thoughtful astronomers have known that for a long time.

What kind of assistance do amateur astronomers give to professionals? How do amateurs spend their time out under the stars? What are some of the remarkable things they see? And what kinds of thoughts and feelings do they have out there in the vast night? Let's answer those questions a bit by seeing what a pair of teenage amateur astronomers might experience on one interesting clear evening when they go out to see what the conditions in the sky are like.

Even before the sun sets, the amateur astronomers—we'll call them Bob and Sue—see that clouds have produced "halo phenomena," strange patches of colorful light and an arc of colors like an upside-down rainbow high over the sun. Halo phenomena are caused by reflection and refraction of sunlight in ice crystals in the clouds. Besides good astronomers, who watch the sky both day and night, whether it is clear or cloudy, few people in the world notice these spectacular wonders above their heads. Of course, Sue and Bob themselves probably just stumbled on the halo phenomena while trying to see if the clouds were moving out, that is, if the night would be clear. But their sky watching is bound to pay off with all kinds of bonuses like this colorful display.

After noting startling distortions of the sun as it sets, Sue and Bob see a huge area of vivid pink light appear partway up the western sky. This is a special twilight glow, which they suspect is caused by the high-altitude haze from a volcano that erupted on the other side of the world months ago. If they note carefully what time it disappears, this information could actually be of help to professional scientists studying our atmosphere.

Finally, the whole sky is beginning to get really dark. Our amateur astronomers are ready to bring out a small telescope and set it up, letting it cool down to the temperature of the now slightly chilly air. (Until it cools down, the difference between its temperature and the air's could create turbulence and therefore unsteady images.)

Bob and Sue will use the telescope a lot this evening, but they will also do a lot of observing with just their naked eyes—that is, their eyes without any binoculars or telescope. They know that there are many wonders up there in the heavens that are actually seen better with the naked eye than with a telescope. They prove this to themselves again by seeing in one naked-eye glance the entire majesty of the Big Dipper in the northeast (no telescope could fit that entire Dipper into its field of view), then the whole noble group of constellations surrounding mighty Orion the Hunter. More proof of what the naked eye can see? Over in the southwest two bright planets hang near each other in an event called a "conjunction"—but tonight they aren't close enough together to fit into the telescope's view. Nor could a telescope capture the two planets together with the entire intricate tree line they hang over, a beautiful scene.

Suddenly, a bright meteor—what is sometimes called a "shooting star"—races across the sky and then is gone. The whole spectacular journey of that meteor across the sky could be captured only by the wide viewing range of the naked eye. (On some nights of the year, Sue and Bob will be able to watch dozens of meteors each hour in one of the year's best meteor showers—and if they do, their counts of the meteors will once again be of value to science, besides being thrilling and fun.)

Now the sky is completely dark, and it's time for the telescope to show the wonders it can reveal—not necessarily better than the naked-eye wonders, just different.

Our amateur astronomers turn their telescope on one of the planets in conjunction, Saturn. There is the butterscotch-colored globe and the chillingly sharp and perfect rings—a live view of this showpiece of the solar system, which in many ways is better than the finest photographs of it you could see in a book. After several minutes of gazing, Sue and Bob swing the tube of the telescope around to turn it on another planet, Mars. The image of this orange world looks a little shaky— but images are always less steady when we gaze at an object through the longer pathway of trembling air down low in the sky. Later on, when Mars is higher, they will study it more carefully and sketch it, hoping to see some of the dark surface markings and one of the polar ice caps or the clouds around it. There's a chance they might also see the golden patch of a giant Martian dust storm, which they could make sketches of to send to scientists studying Mars. The scientists could use that information to learn how to better protect our astronauts when they eventually go to visit that harsh but beautiful world.

A look with the naked eye high overhead shows our friends that, as predicted, the variable star Algol is indeed varying its brightness tonight—experiencing a dramatic dimming. What less well-known variable stars may they start watching in the months ahead—seeing how bright those stars are on different nights—while no one else in the world, or at least no professional astronomer, is watching?

Now it's time to turn the telescope on a double star, this one a blue sapphirelike star almost touching a golden gem. In the same constellation, Andromeda, Bob and Sue put the telescope on the amazing Great Galaxy (also known as "M31"). A fascinating smudge of light to the naked eye, in the telescope the galaxy shows its intense center, its little companion galaxies, its hint of a dark lane which helps prove it is actually a pinwheel of stars, hundreds of billions of them (Figure 1-1).

Next our amateurs admire the Pleiades star cluster—the lovely Seven Sisters—which has been mentioned in the Bible and Greek mythology, is pictured in stylized form on a brand of automobile, and has played a role in deciding when Halloween and other holidays are to be held (Figure 1-2). This cluster is probably most beautiful with the naked eye or binoculars, but Sue and Bob look at it in their telescope too to see if they can detect any trace of the glowing gases from which these young stars were born, in the last days when the dinosaurs walked the Earth.

Not finding the Pleiades gas tonight, our amateur astronomers move the telescope over to a cloud of gas that any telescope can show on almost any night—the brilliant Great Nebula in Orion. This green, intricate fan of star-dusted radiance is a place where new stars are being born right now.

As Sue steps back from yet another view of the Great Nebula and glances around the sky, she and Bob look east and see the glow of a distant city. Much of the

Figure 1-1. *Left:* The Andromeda galaxy, M31, lies over 2 million light-years away from us, but can be seen easily with the unaided eye on a clear country night.

Figure 1-2. *Right:* The Pleiades star cluster (referred to in star lore as "The Seven Sisters") is a group of young stars whose brightest members make a lovely sight on an autumn or winter night.

light coming from that city—and many others—is un-necessary, wasting electricity and costing all of us money. At the same time this unneeded light spoils the view of the universe for many thousands of people within a few dozen miles of the city. Tomorrow, Bob and Sue will write letters to inform local politicians that laws have been passed against this "light pollution" in other parts of the United States and to describe how everybody will win if states and cities work together to eliminate the problem.

But it wasn't the light pollution but a natural source of light that made our amateur astronomers look to the east—it's the moon coming up. Its brightness means that the whole sky will lighten and it will be more difficult to see faint stars and nebulas. Sue and Bob therefore decide to look at Mars and sketch what they see, turn their telescope on the moon, and then call it a night. This is not the first time our young astronomers have explored the moon, but as they gaze on its stark moun-tains and craters, on places where our Apollo astronauts walked, they thrill again to the undisputed magnifi-cence of Earth's fair natural satellite.

In an hour or two of one evening—from a yard that could be yours—our amateur astronomers have experi-enced halo phenomena, a sunset, twilight glows, a me-teor, constellations, a conjunction, planets, a variable star, a double star, a galaxy, a star cluster, a nebula, city skyglow, and close-ups of the moon. For much of this tour, they needed nothing but unaided eyes and knowledge about what to look for. And tomorrow, weather permitting, a brand-new adventure awaits them in the heavens.

Tools for the Amateur Astronomer

It's clear from Chapter One's adventure of the amateur astronomers Sue and Bob that many wonders of the heavens are actually best seen with the naked eyes.

Nevertheless, when someone mentions "the tools of the astronomer," you probably think immediately of a telescope. And if you want to become an amateur astronomer, you may feel you should get a telescope right away. But if you do you will be making a mistake. A beginner should first learn how to identify some of the planets and constellations, and find out how he or she likes being out under the stars for long periods of time.

Think about it: You spend hundreds of dollars and purchase a telescope. Then you go and discover you don't know what to look for up there. Which one of those hundreds of points of light might be Saturn? Which is a double star or has a star cluster near it? When will the moon be out tonight? If you have all these questions you can't answer, you are going to become very frustrated. Since learning to use a telescope properly takes time and patience, you will probably have some trouble with the instrument at first. Many beginners who don't know the basics of astronomy when they buy a telescope simply get annoyed and give up. The telescope is put aside, perhaps never to be used again—which is a great shame.

To avoid these problems, don't buy a telescope until you have learned what astronomy is all about by reading this book and observing the night sky with your naked eyes, then maybe with binoculars. What if you already have a telescope? Then still try our naked-eye projects. A telescope is only as good as the eye and mind that go with it. So if you train your eyes and mind—if you develop those tools of the astronomer first—then the telescope will deliver for you all the wonders it can.

THE EYES

You might think that no one needs to tell you how to use your eyes. But in astronomy there are special techniques of seeing which will help you immensely. But apart from special techniques, keep this in mind: one important way to use the eyes in astronomy is *often*. The more you go out to look, the more you will see. And the more actual hours of time you put into observing sky sights, the more skillful an observer you are likely to become.

The first important technique of vision for amateur astronomers is using *dark adaptation*. When you go outside from the brightly lit indoors at night, your eyes need time to adjust to the darkness before you can really start seeing many of the fainter stars. After about ten or twenty minutes you will notice a great improvement in your sensitivity to faint light in the sky, and after that a smaller but definite improvement. There is actually a chemical process going on in the "rod" cells in your eyes' retinas that increases their ability to detect dim light.

If you have to observe with a lot of bright streetlights or other artificial lights around you, or you live in a big city where the sky is aglow from misdirected artificial lighting, then this "dark adaptation" will only go so far—your eyes will not become as capable of seeing faint objects as they would out at a very dark country location. But if the night is dark at all around you, try not to spoil your adaptation. Never point a flashlight in your own eyes or another person's while out observing. If the light shines in a person's eyes for more than a moment their dark adaptation will be spoiled and it will take many minutes before their eyes regain the same level of sensitivity.

As a matter of fact, even looking down at the star map your flashlight is shining on may reverse your dark adaptation quite a bit. Many amateur astronomers solve this problem by putting some kind of red filter on their flashlight (red cellophane held on with a rubber band may do the job). Why red? Because the rods in your retina are not very sensitive to red—seeing it will not interfere with the chemical process and spoil your dark adaptation.

Another important technique for seeing fainter objects at night is *averted vision*. The greatest concentration of the rods in your retinas is slightly off to the sides from where you direct your gaze. In other words, to make a faint star look brighter you should direct your stare slightly to either side of it. You'll be amazed how well this technique works, and you'll find that you quickly get better at using it.

Some other points about using your eyes in astronomy are plain common sense. For instance, it's very important to rest your eyes at least every few minutes. Try not to stare too long continuously at one object.

THE SKY CONDITIONS

How could the sky conditions be considered a tool of the amateur astronomer? In this way: The knowledgeable observer judges what the sky is like that night and knows what kinds of observations are best to try. Then he or she can use those conditions to get the most out of that night's observing.

A night with bright moonlight is not a good time, or a place with much glow from city lights a good place, to look for faint stars, galaxies, or nebulae. It might be a fine time or place for looking at details on the globes of the planets through a telescope, or at certain features on the moon. The two other sky conditions which are most important along with darkness of your sky are called "transparency" and "seeing."

Transparency simply means how transparent the air is, how much light it lets through from the heavenly objects—in other words, how clear the air is. Just because a sky has no clouds in it, by the way, does not mean it is very transparent: there may be haze in the air that will prevent you from detecting any but the brightest stars that night. When the daytime sky is a deep blue, the nighttime sky is very transparent: such a night is the perfect time to try to see faint stars and other dim objects.

"Seeing" is how steady the images of objects in the sky are, which depends on how calm or turbulent the atmosphere above you is. On a night of good "seeing," when the atmosphere is calm, stars don't twinkle as much, double stars can be easily split, much fine detail may be made out on the moon and planets. Bad "seeing" is caused by turbulence in the atmosphere, but that does not have to mean that the wind is blowing around you: often, the turbulence is many miles above you, making the stars dance with twinkling, making the image of a lunar crater or planet in the telescope look blurry and wavery. And remember that "seeing" always tends to be worse lower in the sky, because there you are looking through a longer pathway of atmosphere.

Sometimes transparency may be good and "seeing" bad, or the opposite: on hazy summer nights we can't see very faint objects (the atmosphere is not very transparent) but the atmosphere may be very still and thus "seeing" may be good for observing bright double stars and planetary features with a telescope.

STAR MAPS, STAR ATLASES, AND PLANISPHERES

As an amateur astronomer you need maps of the heavens to help find whichever of thousands of objects you are looking for. But there's a lot to consider when you choose maps, and some very special kinds of maps to use.

Figures 2-1 to 2-4 are some basic star maps for all seasons of the year. But as you progress as an amateur astronomer, you will want to look for maps that are more sophisticated—or, really, we should say, maps which show stars down to a greater faintness (thus more stars) and show a larger number of special objects (star clusters, nebulas, galaxies) to hunt for. When choosing any star map, check to see how many stars it shows and whether it shows constellations as large as you would want them (especially for viewing out in the dark with your red-filtered flashlight).

Of course, you need some knowledge to be able to understand the symbols and customs of star maps and star atlases. You need to know about special symbols which represent the "scientific names" of stars. And you especially need to know how to understand the system of "celestial coordinates"—the equivalent of latitude and longitude in the sky. (Information about these things can be found in Figure 3-2 of this book.)

But there's a special kind of star map you should also know about: the *planisphere* (sometimes also called a "star finder" or "star wheel"). A planisphere is a plastic or cardboard wheel which you can rotate to show what stars are in the sky at any hour of any date in the year. Each planisphere has instructions with it (usually on it), but the basic idea is to rotate the wheel until the date on the outside part of the wheel matches up with a time of the night printed on an unmoving part of the planisphere. The planisphere is meant to be held above you with the part on top that says "north" pointed in that direction.

CAMERA

These days, amateur astronomers are taking photographs as beautiful as the professionals do—in some cases, more beautiful, because professional astronomers are more concerned with the information which an image contains. But good astrophotography using a telescope requires a lot of time and practice, and a fair amount of equipment. This book will be limited to discussion of the equipment and techniques you need to do just the most basic astrophotography—without a telescope. Even though astrophotography with just a tripod may be basic, it still can produce some of the best views possible of a number of sky sights.

All you require is a 35mm SLR camera (an Instamatic is *not* useful for astrophotography), a tripod, a roll of film, and a cable release. The camera you use must have a shutter that can be kept open for a number of seconds (this is usually done by switching the camera to its B setting—now you manually control when the shutter closes). The tripod can be of any kind—as long as it is sturdy. The roll of film will usually be a "fast" film—one that has a high ISO number—for shooting star scenes. ISO 200 or 400 is fine, but you can also experiment with the new very fast films with speeds of 1600 and even 3200. These very fast films tend to produce pictures that are more "grainy," with objects looking a

Winter

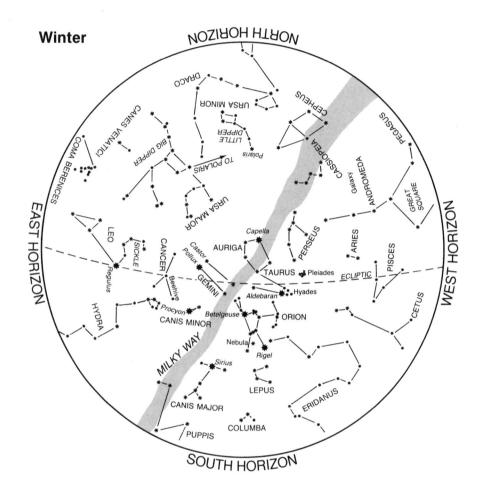

Figure 2-1. The starry sky on winter evenings

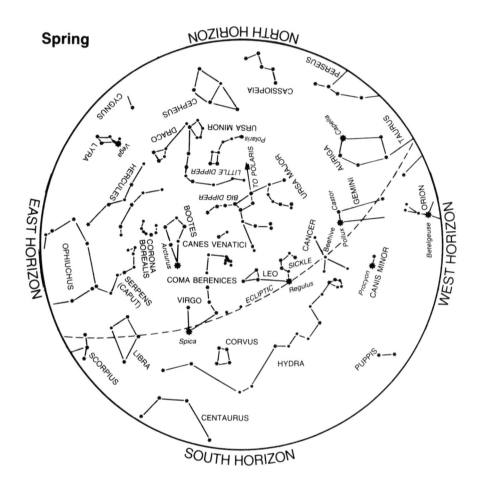

Spring

Figure 2-2. The starry sky on spring evenings

Summer

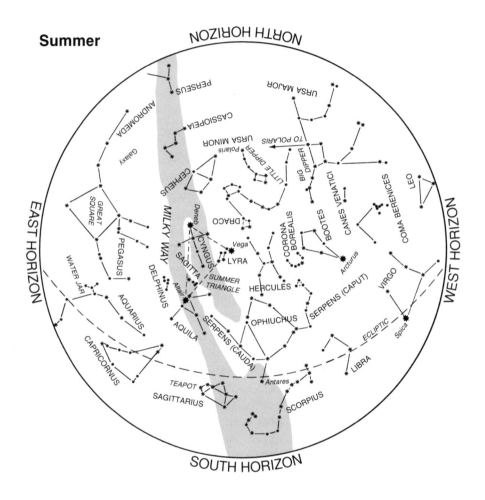

Figure 2-3. The starry sky on summer evenings

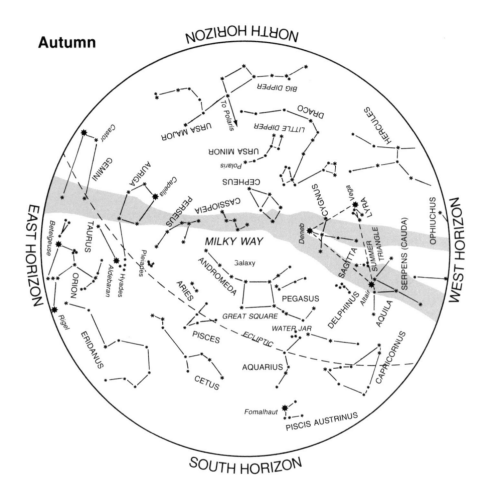

Figure 2-4. The starry sky on autumn evenings

bit fuzzy, but the number of stars they can record in a 10-second or 20-second exposure is amazing.

The cable release is a device (cost: just a few dollars) which enables you to open and close the camera shutter from the end of a little cable—in other words, without having to touch the button on the camera. This is important because touching the camera itself could shake it enough to ruin your photo.

To photograph a starry scene, leave the shutter open 10, 20, 30 seconds or more (how long will depend on what part of the sky you are shooting and how much moonlight, twilight, or city light glow is in the sky). The goal is usually to get a photo that shows as many stars as possible (see Figure 2-5). Why not leave the shutter open much longer? Because the rotation of the Earth causes the star to move from west to east across the sky and this movement will be picked up and elongate the otherwise beautiful little dot of the star on your picture. Of course, if you leave your shutter open for minutes you get the stars appearing in your photos as long streaks of light—"star trails"—a sight that is beautiful in its own right (try it!).

BINOCULARS

But you still want to buy a telescope? Why not first use those portable, far less expensive pairs of small telescopes—binoculars.

Few people realize that binoculars can show you hundreds of features on the moon, dozens of star clusters and galaxies, and far wider views than any you will get in telescopes.

There are many different types of binoculars, and several good books which go into great detail about how

Figure 2-5. Amateur astronomer Ray Maher took this photograph showing vast numbers of stars in a section of the Milky Way band.

to select and use them in astronomy (see "For Further Reading" for my own choice of the best). But there are some basics about binoculars that everyone should learn from the start.

First of all is what those numbers on the binoculars mean! When you see "7×35" on a pair, what information is being presented?

The "7×" refers to the magnifying power—that is,

the binoculars make objects look seven times bigger. The "35" refers to the diameter of the primary lenses (the big pieces of glass in the binoculars), measured in millimeters (mm). Since 1 inch equals about 25 mm, a 35mm lens is a little less than 1½ inches across.

What other sizes of binoculars can you get besides 7 × 35? Which is the best for amateur astronomers?

There are binoculars that magnify 10× or even 20×. Unfortunately, this is still not enough magnification to give close-up views of the planets. Also, when the magnification gets up to about 10× you will find there is a problem: the field of view you see through them is not as wide and therefore you have trouble holding the binoculars steady enough to keep the object you want in view. Of course, you could mount the 10× binoculars on a tripod to keep them steady. But it will still be a bit hard to get the object in sight in the first place, and the whole setup is much less portable than binoculars that can hang around your neck on a strap. All things considered, 7× binoculars (or the less common 8×) are the best all-around ones for amateur astronomers.

But what should the second number, the diameter of the primary lens, be? Here what you want is the widest lens you can get without making the binoculars too heavy. There are 10×80, 11×80 and 20×80 binoculars (there are reasons why 7× does not work with 80mm) but all are too heavy and high magnifying to use well without a tripod (they are also expensive—they are usually bought as second binoculars for special purposes by experienced amateur astronomers). On the other hand, 7×35 binoculars are even less heavy than 7×50s, but the light-gathering power is a little weak. Binoculars 7×35 with the size are really better for daytime observing, such as bird-watching, where you have a reasonable amount of sunlight to work with. The 7×50 is a very common size of binoculars and really is about the best all around for use in astronomy.

TELESCOPES

If you don't have a telescope and are hungry to buy one, ask yourself these questions:

Do I know how to locate some of the constellations?

Can I identify at least a few of the planets?

Have I read a little bit about the basics of astronomy?

Have I tried going out a lot to observe with the unaided eye, and do I find that I enjoy it?

Have I tried using binoculars for astronomy?

If you answered no to most of these questions, you may not be ready for a telescope.

But let's suppose you answered yes to most of them and that you either have a telescope or have a chance to buy one and decide to do it. What are some of the things you need to know to select the best telescope or to use the one you have properly?

First, consider what all telescopes have in common. Each telescope must have *optics*—the lenses and/or mirrors which will give you a brighter image of objects in the sky. The telescope must also have at least one eyepiece (also called an *ocular*), a small assembly of lenses that magnifies the image in the telescope by a certain amount. Finally, you need some kind of tube or other structure to put the optics in and a mount of some kind to support the entire tube assembly.

So all telescopes have some things in common. But there are also major differences between the three most important types.

The three major types are the refractor, reflector, and catadioptric telescope (Figure 2-6). The refractor telescope uses lenses and is looked straight through; the reflector uses mirrors and is normally looked into on the side of the upper end of the tube; the catadioptric uses

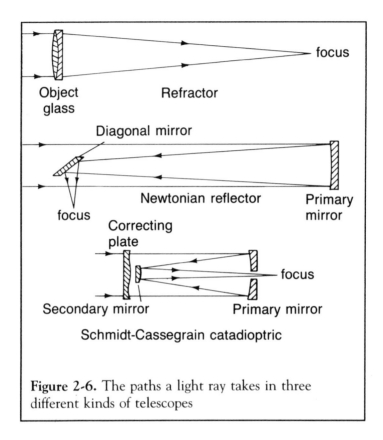

Figure 2-6. The paths a light ray takes in three different kinds of telescopes

lenses and mirrors and is normally looked into at the bottom.

The big question, of course, is which of these types of telescopes is best for you? The answer depends on what your needs and your location are like, and on another big question: how much money can you afford to spend?

If you have less than $200 to spend, many astronomy experts would advise that you just buy binoculars and wait until you have more money. They think that you can't get a very good telescope for that price, and they are probably right. However, I would suggest that one of the cheaper refractors—the kind that you usually see in a department store—could be of acceptable quality for a beginner, if you are careful to check for certain things.

What do you look for? The telescope should be mounted firmly—don't buy it if the image in it shakes for more than just a second or two when you touch the telescope. The telescope should obviously be returnable within a reasonable period of time (preferably at least a month) in case you find out that there is something wrong with the optics. The atmosphere above us is unsteady on some nights, and this may be the reason you don't get a sharp view of the moon or stars the first time you try out your telescope. Do be sure to use the eyepiece that gives lowest magnification first (that should give your sharpest view). But if you are doing everything right according to the instructions that come with the telescope and after trying several nights can't get very sharp images of the moon and other objects, then you should return the telescope.

What size of telescope should you expect to get for less than $200? The important number to notice is the diameter of the primary lens (the big piece of glass). In inexpensive telescopes this will usually be either 50mm (about 2 inches) or 60mm (a little less than $2\frac{1}{2}$ inches). The 60mm is more desirable—the wider your lens, the more light it can gather.

Don't be misled by claims that a telescope can give you superhigh magnification. You can get 400× or 500× with a tiny telescope if you use certain kinds of eyepieces. But it won't matter: with such a small telescope, your images at that high a magnification will be hopelessly blurred. The magnifying power you can suitably use with it depends, just as the all-important light-gathering ability does, on the width of your primary lens (or primary mirror): again, the wider, the better.

The rule is that even when the atmosphere is steady

the most magnification you can use is about 50× for each inch of your lens's or mirror's diameter. In other words, since 50mm is about 2 inches, such a telescope will give decent images only up to a magnification of about 2 times 50×, which is 100×. A telescope with a 6-inch primary mirror could supply a maximum useful magnification of 6 times 50×, which is 300×. Even these figures really apply only to sky objects which bear magnification well, like double stars or Saturn. Most astronomical objects are best seen with somewhat lower magnification, which tends to make them look brighter and sharper. Remember: the objects in the heavens are faint, so light-gathering ability is usually much more important than magnification.

Even for less than $200 a telescope should come with several eyepieces and—this is quite important—a *finderscope*. The finderscope is a little telescope mounted on the main one that gives you a wider view than the main telescope, much like binoculars would. This is very important because the field of view of the main telescope is so narrow that you would have trouble locating whatever little point of light you're trying to see in that huge sky.

But what if you have more than $200 to spend? In the $200 to about $800 range, your best choice will probably be a reflector telescope. A 3-inch or 4-inch refractor (that is, a refractor with a 3-inch- or 4-inch-wide primary lens) will typically cost far more than a reflector of similar size.

With a larger telescope, the whole question of what kind of mount you use and how portable the telescope is becomes crucial (Figure 2-7). An *equatorial mount* is a kind which lets you follow the nightly motion of sky objects more easily. In fact, you can buy one with a *clock drive* that will make the telescope compensate for the Earth's rotation and keep objects in your field of view (without a clock drive, it does become annoying to have to keep moving the tube and getting the thing

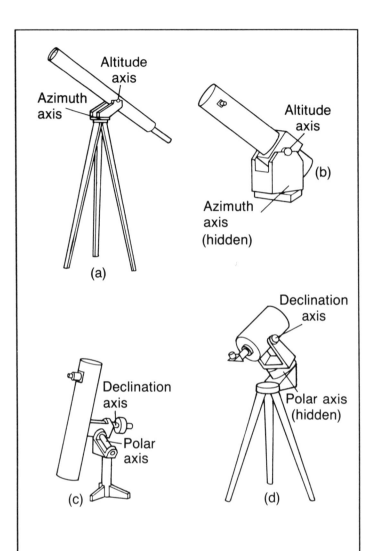

Figure 2-7. Four different types of telescope mountings: (a) a simple altazimuth mounting for a refractor; (b) a Dobsonian altazimuth mounting for a Newtonian reflector; (c) a German equatorial mounting for a Newtonian; (d) a fork equatorial mounting for a catadioptric telescope.

you are looking at in the center of the field of view again).

But equatorial mounts do tend to be heavy. If a telescope and its mount are so heavy you dread moving them, you may not use them much (how strong at lifting are you? Would you normally observe alone, or could you count on a friend's help? Would you need to move the telescope around your yard a lot to get clear views of different parts of the sky?). A telescope with an *altazimuth mount* allows the tube to move just up and down and side to side, not in curves that follow the stars' motions. Therefore, you can't use a clock drive with it and it poses special problems if you eventually decide to try advanced astrophotography. But an altazimuth mount does tend to be lighter and cheaper than an equatorial mount.

In fact, there is a special kind of altazimuth mount, the *Dobsonian mount*, that allows you to get the largest aperture—diameter of main lens or mirror—that you can per dollar. For only about $300 you could have an 8-inch or even 10-inch telescope, for about $500 a 13-inch, for about $1,000 a 17-inch. Remember these are the widths of the mirrors so even with the lightest possible Dobsonian mount these telescopes start getting heavy and awkward. I personally think that the 8-inch Dobsonians are still extremely portable but the larger ones (10-inch, and so on) begin to require more than one person to haul comfortably.

Dobsonian telescopes typically have what we call a small *focal ratio*. The focal ratio is the proportion of the *focal length* to the diameter of the primary mirror or lens. The focal length is the distance from the primary lens or mirror to where it focuses. So the focal ratio of a telescope with an 8-inch-wide mirror and a 32-inch-long focal length would be 32 divided by 8, which is 4 (we would call this an "f/4" focal ratio). An f/4 ratio is a small one, typical for a Dobsonian telescope. That kind of ratio enables you to have a wider field of view—in fact, one type of telescope to consider for $400 or $500 is a small (usually 4-inch or 4¼-inch) one of about f/4 ratio that gives a beautifully wide field of view, rich with stars, and is therefore called a *rich-field telescope*, or RFT. But the drawback of a small focal ratio is that you cannot as easily get high magnifications or sharp views at those magnifications. And that brings up another matter you will have to deal with when you own a reflector: collimation.

Collimation is the alignment of the different lenses or mirrors in an optical system. Your telescope should come with instructions for what is proper collimation and how to achieve it if the optical components ever get out of line. Making the needed adjustments is not necessarily difficult, but you do have to learn how to check the collimation and perform the adjustments if and when they are necessary. Unfortunately, with reflectors these adjustments generally do become necessary, at least from time to time. That is not so much the case with refractors or with catadioptric telescopes—both of which may also need less cleaning because many of the surfaces of their optical components are closed off from the air and dust.

The world's most popular telescopes for amateur astronomers who can afford more than about $800 are 8-inch catadioptric telescopes. One of the advantages of these telescopes is that they are very portable; another is that the companies that make them sell so many that they provide convenient equipment with them to make advanced astrophotography and finding sky objects much easier.

Terms for Touring the Universe

Telescopes and binoculars, planispheres and star atlases, cameras and sketch pads are not the only kinds of tools amateur astronomers use. A very different kind of "tool" is the special language of astronomy.

By "language" I mean the many special words astronomers use to describe objects and phenomena (happenings) in space. In Chapter Two we learned many of the terms connected with telescopes. Now, let's take a two-part tour. First, we'll "visit" the terms astronomers use to describe brightnesses and positions of objects in the sky. Second, we'll tour our entire universe, a survey working outward from the Earth and moon to the farthest reaches of space—all with the help of astronomical terms.

BRIGHTNESSES IN THE SKY

In ancient times, astronomers divided all the stars visible to the naked eye into six classes of brightness, called *magnitudes*. The brightest stars were those of the first magnitude, the next brightest were of the second magnitude, and so on, down to the faintest stars visible, which were of the sixth magnitude.

Finally, in the nineteenth century, astronomers accepted a system by which magnitudes were made more precise and extended to even brighter and even fainter (telescopic) objects. In this reckoning, a difference of one magnitude means that the brighter object is about 2.512 times brighter than the fainter object. Why this odd number? Because 2.512 (really 2.5118 . . .) multiplied by itself five times equals 100: a difference of five magnitudes is 100 times brighter. So a star that is exactly first magnitude, 1.0 (note that we can use decimals for more precise magnitudes) is 100 times brighter than one which is exactly sixth magnitude, 6.0.

The world's biggest telescopes have gotten images of stars and galaxies that are fainter than twenty-fifth magnitude. On the opposite end of things, we have very bright stars of magnitude 0, the brightest star at a negative magnitude of −1.4, Venus at magnitude −4, the full moon at −12.7, and the sun at −26.7.

POSITIONS IN THE SKY

How do astronomers divide up the heavens into manageable sections? How do they measure distances from one point in the heavens to another? How do they precisely identify the location of an object in the heavens? Let's answer these questions one at a time.

How are the heavens divided into sections?
The *constellations* were originally patterns of stars, and there was much disagreement about which were the official constellations and which stars belonged to which constellation. But early in the twentieth century astronomers adopted eighty-eight official constellations, and the stricter definition of *constellation* became the demarcated sections of the heavens which contained the old patterns. A listing of all the official constellations is found in Appendix 2.

Some of the most famous constellations are those

Table 1 Traditional Constellations
of the Zodiac

Aries the Ram
Taurus the Bull
Gemini the Twins
Cancer the Crab
Leo the Lion
Virgo the Virgin
Libra the Scales
Scorpius the Scorpion *
Sagittarius the Archer
Capricornus the Sea Goat (or Goat-Fish)
Aquarius the Water Bearer
Pisces the Fishes

* The sun actually spends less time in Scorpius than in the dimmer constellation Ophiuchus.

that make up the *zodiac*—the band of constellations in which the sun, moon, and planets are always located (Table 1). Long ago, many more people believed in astrology than do today. Astrology claims that what constellation of the zodiac the sun, moon, or planets are in can have an effect on people's lives and luck. Now we know that the claims of astrology are false. Why are the sun, moon, and planets confined to the same band of constellations? The reason is that the Earth, moon, and planets are all orbiting the sun in almost the same plane. The midline of the zodiac is the *ecliptic*, the sun's apparent yearly path through the constellations. We say "apparent" because it is really the Earth that is going around the sun; the sun merely looks like it is circling around us, around our heavens.

Although some stars have proper names which are still widely used, every star has an official "scientific name." For most of the brighter naked-eye stars this consists of a letter of the Greek alphabet and the possessive form of its constellation's name. Thus the first-named star in Leo is Alpha (first letter of the Greek alphabet) Leonis. The letters ought to be applied to stars within a constellation in order of brightness, but there are many exceptions to this rule (for instance, the Alpha star is not always the brightest within a constellation).

How are distances measured from one point to another in the heavens?

These distances are given in *angular measure:* that is, they are measured in angles that are fractions of the 360° of a full circle—the full circle we would travel if we went all the way across the sky and around the world under our feet. Half of this 360° is the 180° from one *horizon* (meeting place of land or sea and the sky) through the *zenith* (overhead point) to the opposite horizon. The distance from horizon to zenith is 90°. And we can measure the distance between any two stars or planets in degrees. In fact, there's an easy way to figure out roughly how many degrees long any distance in the sky is: hold your fist out at arm's length and measure the distance in number of fists. At arm's length, everyone's fist is roughly 10° wide (Figure 3-1).

Very small distances or dimensions, tiny fractions of a degree, are measured in *minutes of arc* and *seconds of arc.* One degree contains 60 minutes of arc (represented by the symbol ′). One minute of arc contains 60 seconds of arc (represented by the symbol ″). The sun and moon both appear about $\frac{1}{2}$° or 30′ wide. Jupiter appears about 40″ wide on the average.

How is the position of an object in the heavens precisely defined?

Astronomers use a system of *celestial coordinates,* which are given in terms of *right ascension (RA)* and

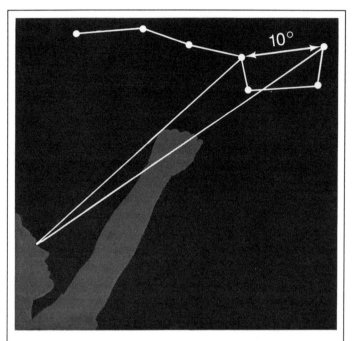

Figure 3-1. Your fist held out at full-arm's length is about 10 degrees across, and can be used for estimating angular distances in the sky. The width of the top of the Big Dipper's bowl is about 10 degrees.

declination. An imaginary celestial sphere of the heavens has poles and equator right over those of Earth, with RA in the heavens corresponding to longitude on the Earth, and declination in the heavens corresponding to latitude on the Earth. RA, however, is measured in 24 "hours" (divided into minutes and seconds) which are counted eastward in the heavens from the 0^h line of RA. That line runs through the vernal equinox point in the heavens (the place where the sun is located in the heavens when spring begins in Earth's northern hemisphere). Declination is measured in degrees, minutes, and seconds, like latitude, but declinations north of the celestial equator are preceded by a plus sign (+) and those south of the equator by a minus sign (−).

Figures 3-2 and 3-3 show how the imaginary celestial sphere looks and why from the latitudes of the U.S. there are *north circumpolar* stars (such as those of the Dippers) going around the north celestial pole in small enough circles to never be cut off by the horizon, which thus never rise or set.

EARTH AND MOON

Now we begin our "tour" of the terms describing the universe, starting out from home.

Our world, the Earth, rotates and revolves. *Rotation* is the spinning around of an astronomical body. The Earth makes one full rotation each twenty-four hours, a period of time we call a *day*. Many other objects in space take more time or less time than Earth does to rotate: we say that their "rotation periods" are longer or shorter than Earth's.

Revolution is the circling or orbiting of one astronomical body around another. The Earth revolves around the sun. It makes one full revolution in about $365\frac{1}{4}$ days, a period of time we call a *year*. (To keep our calendar accurate we have to add an extra day, a "leap day," every fourth year, or "leap year," which is 366 days long instead of 365).

Earth has one natural satellite or moon, which we call the moon, and which shines by reflecting to us sunlight off part of it or all of it that faces Earth. The word *lunar* means "having to do with the moon, or belonging to the moon."

The amount of the moon facing us that we see lit is called the moon's *phase*. The four most important phases occur in this order: new moon, first quarter moon, full moon, and last quarter moon. *New moon* is the phase

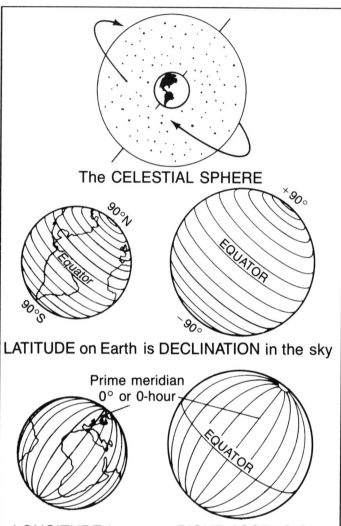

The CELESTIAL SPHERE

LATITUDE on Earth is DECLINATION in the sky

LONGITUDE becomes RIGHT ASCENSION

Figure 3-2. You can locate a star using the celestial sphere, right ascension, and declination. Right ascension and declination are essentially projections in the sky of the lines of latitude and longitude on the Earth's surface.

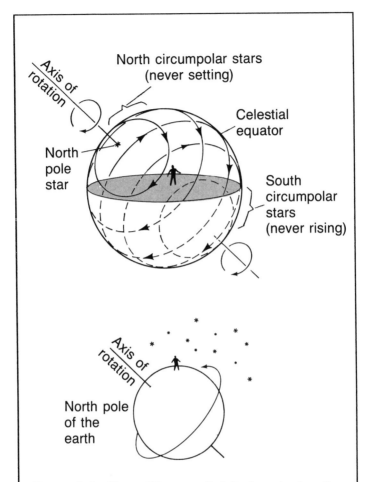

North circumpolar stars
(never setting)

Axis of rotation

Celestial equator

North pole star

South circumpolar stars
(never rising)

Axis of rotation

North pole of the earth

Figure 3-3. *Above:* The so-called "celestial sphere" *appears* to rotate around us once a day from east to west. From the perspective of an observer in the northern hemisphere, the north circumpolar stars never set and the south circumpolar stars never rise. *Below:* In reality, the Earth rotates from west to east. From the observer's perspective, the sun, stars, and planets appear to move from east to west.

when none of the moon pointed toward us is lit (thus it is invisible). *Crescent moon* is a phase in which some of the moon is lit, but less than half of it. The first time after new moon when we see the lunar face half-lit is called *first quarter moon* (because the moon has then completed the first quarter of its way around its month-long journey from one new moon to the next). *Gibbous moon* is a phase in which more than half the moon but less than all of it is lit. *Full moon* is of course the phase at which all of the moon facing us is lit. The second and last time since new moon that we see the lunar face half-lit is called *last quarter moon* (because the moon is beginning the last quarter of its monthlong journey from one new moon to the next).

How long does it take for the moon to revolve (circle or orbit) around the Earth? It takes a month (the word originally might have been spelled "moonth"!). But what kind of month? Most months on our calendar are either 30 or 31 days long. The two most important kinds of lunar month are shorter. The *sidereal month* is how long it takes for the moon to return to about the same place in relation to the distant background of stars behind it. The sidereal month is about $27\frac{1}{3}$ days long. However, because the Earth is moving onward in its own orbit around the sun, the moon takes a little longer to get back to the same place in relation to Earth and sun and thus a bit longer to go from one full moon to the next, one new to the next, etc. So this *synodic month*—the period from one occurrence of a lunar phase until its next occurrence—is about $29\frac{1}{2}$ days.

How long does it take for the moon to rotate? The same amount of time as it takes for the moon to go from one phase to its next occurrence: one synodic month. This means that the moon always keeps just about the same side of itself pointed toward Earth.

What features do we see on the moon? Even with the naked eye we can see dark markings on the moon which are called *maria* (MAH-ree-uh)—the singular is *mare* (MAH-ray). *Mare* is the Latin word for "sea" because people used to believe that the dark markings on the moon were oceans. We now know that there is no water on the surface of the moon and that the maria are large gray plains of hardened lava.

A closer look at the moon with binoculars and telescope shows holes of all sizes on the moon's surface called *craters.* Other features on the moon include mountains, special valleys called *rills,* and streaks of bright dust extending from some craters, called *rays.* Almost all the lunar features except rays are seen most sharply when they are outlined by their own prominent shadows, and this occurs when they are near the line separating light and dark, day and night on the moon—the line called the terminator.

The moon's orbit around the Earth is not a perfect circle. The point in the moon's orbit farthest from Earth is called *apogee.* The point in the moon's orbit nearest to Earth is called *perigee.*

ECLIPSES OF THE MOON AND SUN

When the Earth, moon, and sun get into a nearly perfect line in space, an eclipse occurs. An *eclipse* is either a hiding or a shadowing of one astronomical body by another.

An eclipse of the sun, or *solar eclipse,* happens when the moon passes between the Earth and the sun (Figure 3-4). A solar eclipse can take place only at new moon, but such an eclipse does not take place at every new moon. An eclipse of the moon, or *lunar eclipse,* happens when the Earth comes between the sun and the moon, so that the shadow of the Earth is cast upon the moon. A lunar eclipse can take place only at full moon, but such an eclipse does not take place at every full moon.

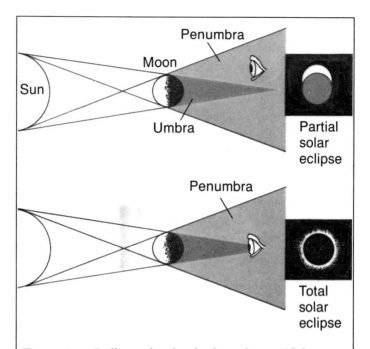

Figure 3-4. Different kinds of solar eclipses. If the eye is in the penumbra (outer shadow) of the moon, the observer sees a *partial solar eclipse*. If the eye is in the umbra (central shadow) of the moon, the observer sees a *total solar eclipse*. An annular eclipse occurs when the moon is farther than usual and its umbra does not quite reach the observer's eye.

There are several kinds of solar eclipses. If only part of the sun is covered, the event is a *partial solar eclipse*. If all of the sun is covered, the event is a *total solar eclipse*. Sometimes, the moon may move directly in front of the sun but be especially far out from Earth in its orbit and therefore appear not quite big enough to cover the sun. When this happens, we witness an *annular solar eclipse*, in which a ring, or *annulus* (the Latin word

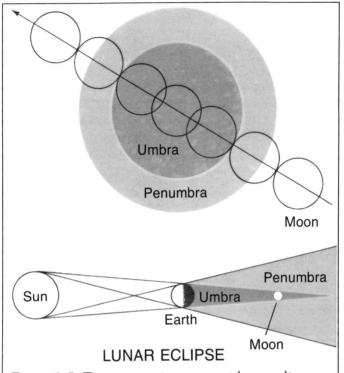

Umbra

Penumbra

Moon

Penumbra

Sun

Umbra

Earth

Moon

LUNAR ECLIPSE

Figure 3-5. Two perspectives on total lunar eclipses: (a) how moon passes through cross-section of Earth's umbra (central shadow) and penumbra (outer shadow) in the sky; (b) side-view in space of such an eclipse (not drawn to scale).

for "ring") of the sun's blazing surface is left uncovered and shines out from around the moon's dark form.

There are also several kinds of lunar eclipse (Figure 3-5). The Earth and other objects really have two parts to their shadow: an inner, darker part called the *umbra* (a word which means "shade" in Latin—an "umbrella" is a "little shade") and an outer, less dark part around the umbra called the *penumbra* (Latin for "almost umbra"). An eclipse in which the moon passes only through the Earth's penumbra is called a *penumbral lunar eclipse*. An eclipse in which only part of the moon goes into the umbra is called a *partial lunar eclipse*. An eclipse in which all of the moon goes into the umbra is called a *total lunar eclipse*.

THE SOLAR SYSTEM

Now we leave the Earth and moon and travel out to meet the other members of the sun's family—the family known as the solar system.

The *solar system* is a system made up of a star called the sun and all the objects in space which are dominated by the sun's gravity and therefore revolve (orbit) around the sun. The different kinds of objects besides the sun are planets, moons, asteroids (also called minor planets), meteoroids, and comets.

The Sun • The *sun* is an average-size yellow star but appears tremendously brighter and bigger than other stars because it is many thousands of times closer to us than the others. The word *solar* means having to do with the sun, or belonging to the sun (thus the solar system is the system of objects in space which belongs to the sun).

The blindingly bright surface of the sun is called the *photosphere*. The thin layer of gases just above this which can be glimpsed briefly and colorfully at total eclipses of the sun is the *chromosphere*. The vast region of outer gases which can be seen glowing with a pearly light during a total solar eclipse is the *corona* of the sun.

Sunspots, which occur often, are less hot regions on the sun's surface that appear dark in comparison to the surrounding blaze. *Prominences* are vast streamers of solar material which rise above the surface and may be glimpsed during total solar eclipses. A *solar flare* is an eruption of atomic particles on the sun that strengthens part of the *solar wind*, the outflow of atomic particles from the sun that extends to out beyond Pluto.

Planets, Moons, Rings • The *planets* are the nine large worlds which revolve directly around the sun. The planets in the inner solar system are worlds composed mostly of rock. Earth is one of them (Mercury, Venus, and Mars are the others), and so these worlds are called the *terrestrial planets*. (*Terrestrial* means "of Earth" or "like the Earth"; thus these are the planets most like the Earth.)

The planets in the outer solar system (much farther away from the sun than the terrestrial planets) include the gas giant planets and Pluto. The *gas giant planets*—Jupiter, Saturn, Uranus, and Neptune—are those that are solid inside but have thousands of miles of their outer layers composed of gases. They truly are "giants," ranging from about four to eleven times wider than Earth. What kind of planet is Pluto? Composed of rock and ice, it may be more like Neptune's moon Triton than anything else—but Pluto does revolve directly around the sun and is much bigger than any asteroid and so deserves to be called a planet.

The orbits of the planets are not perfect circles. The point in a planet's orbit (or the orbit of anything revolving around the sun) which is farthest from the sun is called *aphelion*. The point in a planet's orbit which is nearest to the sun is called *perihelion*.

Small worlds that revolve around planets are called *moons* or *satellites* (they are "natural satellites," in contrast to the "artificial satellites" that mankind has launched to orbit around our planet). *Rings* are collections of smaller particles and chunks of ice or dust which revolve around some of the planets in bands.

Asteroids, Meteoroids, Comets • *Asteroids*, also called "minor planets," are rocky bodies which revolve around the sun but are much smaller than the planets. Most asteroids are located between the orbits of Mars and Jupiter. The asteroids range in size from over 600 miles (965 km) wide (far less than half the diameter of the smallest planet) to less than a mile (1.6 km) wide.

Meteoroids are also rocky bodies which revolve around the sun, but they are smaller than asteroids and more widely spread around the solar system. An object could be as much as several hundred yards across and still be called a meteoroid (rather than an asteroid). The smallest meteoroids, called "micrometeoroids," are mere specks too small to see.

Comets are objects composed of ice (mostly frozen water but also other frozen substances) combined with dust and rock (and possibly a rocky core) that release vast clouds of gas and dust when they get close enough to the sun. When far from the sun, a comet is nothing but a frozen mass, called the *nucleus.* If the nucleus gets into the inner solar system, close enough to the sun, the surface ice "sublimes" (goes directly from solid to vapor). Whereas the nucleus may be about 1 to 10 miles (1.6–16 km) across (very rarely, it may be much bigger), the cloud of gas and dust around it may grow to over a million miles (1,600,000 km) wide. The cloud of dust and gas is called the *coma,* and the coma together with the nucleus inside of it are the *head* of the comet. If there is enough dust and gas we may get to see it pushed away from the comet by the solar wind of atomic particles and by the pressure of solar radiation to form a streamer or fan of very thinly spread dust and gas called the *tail* of the comet. Comet tails can be tens of millions of miles long, or even longer.

Many meteoroids are pieces of dust and rock which have been released in comet tails long ago, or broken off from asteroids long ago.

There are two major kinds of comets: *periodic* (or *short-period*) *comets* and *long-period comets.* Periodic comets are those that orbit around the sun in less than 200 years; long-period comets orbit around the sun in more than 200 years. Some long-period comets have orbital periods many thousands of years long, and spend only a year or less of this time far enough into the inner solar system for the sun to thaw them and make them easily visible from Earth. Most of the time they are many times farther out than Pluto on their long, skinny orbits.

Planetary Positions and Appearances as Seen from Earth • We pause on our journey outward to note some of the terms astronomers use to describe the special positions and appearances which planets take on as seen from the viewpoint of our own moving observing platform, the planet Earth.

Some of the most interesting sights occur when one planet passes near another—in our sky, not in space. In space, remember, one planet will always be millions of miles farther away. What has happened is that Earth has moved into a rough line with the other two planets: we merely see the two lie along the same line of sight. We call such an event a conjunction.

A *conjunction* is a meeting of two or more astronomical objects—one planet and another planet, a planet and the moon, the moon or a planet and a star. Technically, the exact moment of conjunction occurs when one of the objects passes due north or due south (or, in rare cases, right in front of!) the other. When the moon or a planet passes right in front of another object, the event is the closest kind of conjunction, an *occultation*. To occult means to hide. (By the way, in a few cases, such as when the moon passes in front of the sun and hides it, we use the term *eclipse* rather than *occultation* to describe one astronomical body hiding another.)

The kinds of views we get of a planet from our observing platform called the Earth also depend greatly on whether the planet is closer to or farther from the sun than the Earth is. The planets closer to the sun than Earth is are the *inferior planets* (by *inferior* we mean lesser in distance, not in quality); the planets farther from the sun than Earth is are the *superior planets* (by *superior* we

47

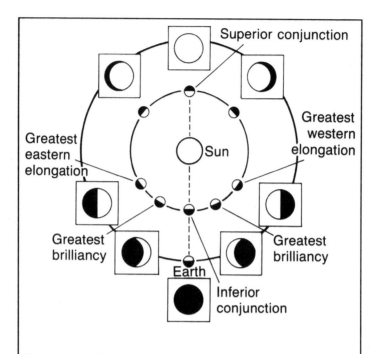

Figure 3-6. The positions and phases of an inferior planet. Phases represent what is seen telescopically from Earth at each of the planet's positions.

mean greater in distance, not in quality). The inferior planets are Mercury and Venus. The superior planets are Mars, Jupiter, Saturn, Uranus, Neptune, and Pluto.

The series of appearances an inferior planet goes through as seen from Earth are much different than those of a superior planet (see Figures 3-6 and 3-7).

Each planet sometimes appears on or near our line of sight with the sun, and is then in *conjunction with the sun* (and not viewable due to the sun's overwhelming brightness). But a superior planet can have a conjunction with the sun only when it is on the far side of the sun from us. An inferior planet can also be in conjunction with the sun when it passes between (or almost

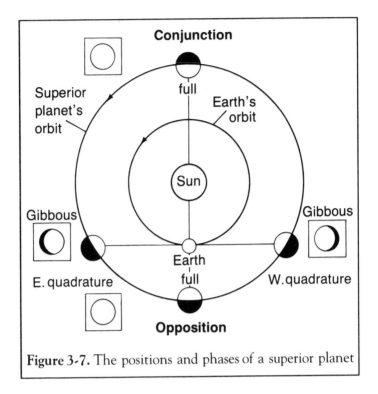

Figure 3-7. The positions and phases of a superior planet

between) Earth and sun—an event called *inferior conjunction* ("inferior" because the distance of the planet from Earth is then less). When an inferior planet is in conjunction with the sun on the far side of the sun from us the event is called *superior conjunction*.

There are also differences between what are the best positions for observing an inferior planet and a superior planet. An inferior planet can be seen only for a few hours (at most) after sunset or before sunrise. This occurs about when the planet is farthest separated from the sun in the sky, which is called *greatest elongation*. For the planet Venus we also note when the planet is at *greatest brilliancy*—which simply means (for all practical purposes) when it is brightest. But a superior planet is brightest (also closest, and biggest in telescopes), and at its best position for us to observe at about the same time. That position, which is called *opposition*, occurs when the planet is opposite the sun in our sky. When it is at opposition, a planet rises at sunset, is visible all night long (highest around midnight), and sets at sunrise.

A final peculiarity about planets' appearances is caused partly by the fact that we observe from a place—Earth—that is itself moving. Most of the time, planets creep slowly (from week to week, month to month, year to year) eastward as seen in relation to the background of distant stars. This is called *direct motion*. It is the true forward motion of the planets in their orbits. For a number of weeks or months each year, however, a planet appears to halt—reach a *stationary point* against the starry background—and then to move westward, backward, which we call *retrograde motion*. The planet reaches another stationary point and then resumes direct motion.

Do planets really halt in their orbits and then start to move backwards through space when we see them retrograde in our sky? No, this is an illusion which occurs because Earth is catching up to a superior planet, or being caught up to by an inferior planet, in their race around their solar orbits. This illusion is something we learn about more fully by observation and experiment on pp. 105–9.

STARS, DOUBLE STARS, AND VARIABLE STARS

Our tour of the universe with terms now takes a giant leap. Venus is (at its closest to Earth) about 100 times farther than the moon. Pluto is (at its closest to Earth) about 100 times farther than Venus gets. But how far is the nearest star other than our own sun? It is about 8,000 times farther away than Pluto! And a few stars visible to the naked eye are 1,000 times farther than the nearest star.

Perhaps the best way possible to visualize how huge the distances are between the stars is by trying the experiment on pp. 112–13, author Guy Ottewell's "Earth as a Peppercorn" model of the solar system.

How many miles is it to Pluto? Almost 3 billion—that's 3,000,000,000 miles (more than 4.8 billion km)—and sometimes farther. How many miles to the nearest star? About 25 trillion miles: 25,000,000,000,000 miles (40 trillion km)!

We don't want to keep writing out such huge numbers when we discuss interstellar ("between the stars") distances, so we use a larger unit of distance. The unit is the light-year. A *light-year* is the distance the fastest thing in the universe, light, travels in one year. Since light travels at about 186,000 miles per second, a light-year is 5.8 trillion miles: 5,800,000,000,000 miles (9.3 trillion km). The distance to the nearest star is 4.3 light-years.

Can we ever travel these great distances in a space-ship? Maybe someday. But we can already travel to the stars by another way—with our imaginations. Let's do it!

Different Kinds of Stars • If we visit many stars, we find that they come in many brightnesses, sizes, masses (total amounts of material, or true weights), and colors.

Earlier in this chapter, we saw how the brightness of stars is rated by magnitude. Actually, however, the brightness that a star seems to show in our sky is only its *apparent magnitude*. Some truly dim stars appear bright in our sky because they are much closer to us than most others; some truly bright stars don't appear so bright because they happen to be especially far away from us. But suppose we could move all stars to a standard distance and compare them all. Then we could see what their true brightnesses were. The *absolute magnitude* of a star is how bright it would look at the standard distance of 10 parsecs, or about 32.6 light-years. Another way to rate the true brightness of stars is to compare them to the sun. We could say that one star was ten times brighter than the sun, another only half as bright as the sun. The true brightness of a star, measured in units of the sun's brightness (sun's brightness = 1) is the *luminosity* of the star. A star ten times brighter than the sun has a luminosity of 10.

Some stars have far less mass than the sun, others far more. Some are much smaller than the sun—no bigger than a planet (or even smaller!)—others are hundreds of times larger. Some stars are yellow like our sun; others are red, orange, white, blue-white. The color of stars relates closely to their surface temperature—red stars are coolest, blue-white stars hottest.

Why are there so many different kinds of stars? One reason is that a star changes during the course of its long, long life, and as we gaze out into space we are seeing stars at many different stages of their lives—young stars, middle-aged stars, very old stars.

Here, let's just define a few of the most famous special types of stars. A *red giant* is an enormous, very massive reddish star with very thin, cool outer layers but so much surface area that it has a great total luminosity. A *blue giant* is a blue-white star much more massive and much larger than our sun, usually smaller than red giants, but with a very hot surface and great luminosity. A *red dwarf* is a small, cool reddish star with very low luminosity and very little mass. A *white dwarf* is a white, extremely hot star even smaller than a red dwarf—in fact, sometimes similar to Earth in size!—but with a fairly large mass (similar to the sun's) and therefore its material crammed into itself incredibly densely.

To get stars even smaller and more densely packed than white dwarfs requires some explosive action. The less devastating kind of star explosion is called a *nova*, an explosion in which perhaps only about 10 percent of the star's mass is blown off into space, leaving a white dwarf star. The far more powerful kind of star explosion is a *supernova*, in which much of a star's mass is blown off and what is left collapses into a neutron star or a black hole.

A *neutron star* is a star that may be as massive as the sun but with all that material collapsed into a ball of subatomic particles no more than 10 or 20 miles (16 or 32 km) across—a star collapsed to the size of a city! Astronomers think that every neutron star may be a *pulsar*—an object which emits pulses of radio waves and sometimes light. But they think that only a small percentage of neutron stars have their magnetic fields oriented so that the bursts of energy reach Earth and enable us to identify them as pulsars.

A *black hole* is a star collapsed so completely that it disappears from sight (it becomes infinitely small!). Its gravity is so strong that nothing, not even light, that comes close enough to it can escape being pulled in by the gravity. Only very massive stars that go supernova end up having their remnants collapse into black holes— or so we think. Actually, astronomers have yet to find absolute proof that black holes exist—though few doubt that they do exist.

Double Stars and Variable Stars • A *double star* is a star which upon closer examination (often with the higher magnification of a telescope) turns out to be two or more stars. If more than two stars are involved, the star system can be called a *multiple star*. A double star may be an *optical double*, a pair of stars which are not really near each other in space but merely happen to lie on almost the same line of sight as seen from Earth (one of the stars might be several times farther away than the other). Most double stars are truly close to each other in space, perhaps even orbiting around each other, and therefore are called *binary stars*. The brighter star in a double star is called the *primary*, the fainter is called the *companion*.

A *variable star* is a star which varies in brightness. The length of time between two occurrences of maximum brightness is called the *period*; the amount of brightness change between minimum and maximum brightness is called the *amplitude*. Some stars vary in brightness because they are binary stars in which one of the stars passes in front of the other, and these are called *eclipsing binaries*. Other variable stars are *intrinsic variables*, which means the stars themselves really do change in brightness, due to internal changes. *Long-period variables* are stars whose periods—which are generally months long—and amplitudes are not always the same each time the star's brightness varies. There are shorter-period variables with very regular (always the same) period and amplitude, the most famous type of which are the *Cepheids*. There are many other types of variable stars.

THE GALAXY, STAR CLUSTERS, AND NEBULAS

A galaxy is a vast gathering of usually billions of stars. When we speak of "the galaxy" we mean our own home galaxy, *the Milky Way*. The Milky Way is shaped like a spiral pinwheel, with a center composed of mostly very old stars and outward curving "spiral arms" composed of mostly young stars, gatherings of stars called star clusters, and clouds of gas and dust called nebulas. Because we are located within the disk of the pinwheel (in one of the spiral arms) we see most of our galaxy as just a band of glow which stretches across the starry sky, and we call this glow the Milky Way. The band is the combined radiance of millions of stars in our galaxy that are too far away to appear as individual points of light to the naked eye.

Star Clusters • A *star cluster* is a kind of collection of stars together in space. It covers more area and contains more stars, usually farther apart, than a multiple star does.

There are two major kinds of star cluster: open clusters (also called "galactic clusters") and globular clusters (Figure 3-8). *Open clusters* are fairly loose collections (they look rather "open"—quite a bit of space is visible between stars) of dozens, hundreds, or even a few thousand stars. Open clusters are found in the spiral arms of our galaxy and often contain young or fairly young stars.

Globular clusters are giant, roundish, and quite concentrated (not loose, not "open") collections of many thousands or even as many as a few million stars. Globular clusters are not confined to the spiral arms or the equatorial disk of our galaxy that we are in; they can also be found high above or below the disk and form a kind of spherical halo around the center of the galaxy (this halo is vast: many globular clusters are much farther from the center of the galaxy than our solar system is, and our solar system may be 30,000 light-years from the center). The stars in globular clusters are all old ones, much like those in the central hub of our pinwheel-shaped galaxy.

Nebulas • A *nebula* is a huge cloud of gas and dust in space. The major kinds are diffuse nebulas (which include emission and reflection nebulas), planetary nebulas, and dark nebulas.

Diffuse nebulas are irregular-shaped clouds of glowing gas and dust. They are the material which will eventually condense to form new stars and perhaps new planets. The pinkish parts of them that are heated enough by young, very hot stars to glow on their own are called *emission nebulas.* The bluish parts of diffuse nebulas which glow only by reflecting the light of nearby stars are called *reflection nebulas.*

Figure 3-8. Photographs of a globular cluster (left) and
an open cluster (right)

Dark nebulas are merely nebulas which are not illuminated. The only way we get to detect them is if they are seen in silhouette in front of a bright nebula or against an area of the sky which is very rich in stars.

Planetary nebulas are often roundish or ring-shaped clouds of glowing gas and dust surrounding a very bright "central star." These nebulas are not the material from which new stars are being born; they are the material an old star has thrown off as it starts dying. We are not sure whether planetary nebulas are usually caused by the type of star explosion called a nova. Why are these nebulas called planetary? Only because in a small telescope many of them appear similar in shape and color (even in apparent size—not real size) to gas giant planets, especially Uranus and Neptune.

Supernova remnants are the gas and dust expelled by the catastrophic supernova explosions of stars. The most famous is called the Crab Nebula.

GALAXIES, QUASARS, AND THE UNIVERSE

The *universe* is the sum total of everything we can physically detect or think we can detect out to the farthest reaches of space.

For the final part of our touring the universe with terms, we must leave our Milky Way galaxy and travel even further. Remember that the nearest star system to our own is about 4.3 light-years away. How big is the Milky Way galaxy? Certainly more than 100,000 light-years across. But how far is the nearest other galaxy? If we don't count small galaxies—including a number which appear to revolve around the Milky Way—the nearest really major galaxy is M31, the Great Andromeda Galaxy. You may remember that we met M31 in Chapter 1. Light from the Great Andromeda Galaxy takes over 2 million years to reach us—which means that M31 is over 2 million light-years away.

Yet, as we shall see, the distance to the edge of the universe is very much greater.

Galaxies and Quasars • A *galaxy* is a vast gathering of usually billions of stars, and our Milky Way galaxy is not the only one. Indeed, we have detected billions of other galaxies. There seem to be three major kinds.

Spiral galaxies, like the Milky Way, are shaped like pinwheels with a central hub of old stars surrounded by spiral arms of young stars, star clusters, and nebulas. *Elliptical galaxies* are round or oval, and resemble the central hubs of spiral galaxies. *Irregular galaxies* are formless, and contain the kind of stars, clusters, and nebulas found in the arms of spiral galaxies.

Quasars are objects believed to be billions of light-years away and thousands of times smaller than galaxies, yet they produce more light and radio waves than galaxies. Perhaps they are the cores of young galaxies, maybe with massive black holes somehow providing the power for the great outpouring of energy.

The Universe and the Big Bang Theory • Astronomers have evidence that the galaxies are all moving away from us—and from each other. The evidence is a change in the location of lines in the spectrum of galaxies which is called a *redshift.* Why are the galaxies fleeing from one another? The *Big Bang theory* argues that all the matter in the universe was once concentrated into a small, supercondensed mass which "exploded," providing an ever-larger space in which matter flew outward to slowly form galaxies, stars, and planets.

How large and how old is the universe? Astronomers think that the farthest reaches of the universe we are capable of detecting may be about 15 billion light-years away. And something like 15 to 20 billion years may have passed since the Big Bang.

Exploring Sky Effects in the Earth's Atmosphere

So far we have studied many of the tools and terms used by the amateur astronomer. Now we are ready to take our knowledge and resources and apply them to our own explorations and investigations of the universe. Let's now begin our adventure of meeting the universe live—as up close and personally as we can.

Astronomical bodies like the sun and moon can take on strange appearances when our view of them is affected by factors in the Earth's atmosphere. The sun and moon can also produce beautiful glows or rings or other patterns of light with the help of raindrops, ice crystals, volcanic haze, or upper-atmosphere gases and Earth's magnetic field. Any amateur astronomer motivated enough to study and admire planets or star clusters will also want to see and learn about rainbows, halos, and twilights.

RAINBOWS, HALO PHENOMENA, CORONAS, AND IRIDESCENT CLOUDS

1. Rainbows. *Study the special features of a rainbow, describing each in detail.*

Rainbows are not common in most climates, but you'll be surprised how much more often you'll see them if you know some of the basics about where and when they occur.

Remember that sunlight and rain are needed to produce a rainbow, but the rain does not have to be falling right where you are located. You might see the rainbow form in a shower several miles east of you late on a summer afternoon. Another important point about when to look for rainbows is that the sun must be fairly low, no more than about 42° (a little over four widths of your fist at arm's length) above the horizon.

And where do you look for the rainbow? In the sky opposite from the sun—more precisely, about 42° from the *antisolar point* (point directly opposite the sun and therefore below the horizon when the sun is above the horizon). The antisolar point is located at the shadow of your head. So search for the first glint of rainbow 42° from that shadow.

What is the rainbow? It is the colored border of the light which is not only reflected back to you by raindrops but also refracted (bent) due to its passage from air to water (the raindrop) and back out to air. The different wavelengths (colors) which make up sunlight are separated because they get refracted in different amounts (some to a greater angle than others).

There's lots more to learn about the rainbow and its strange nature—a rainbow can disappear from the sky while what appears to be its reflection on calm water below still lingers! But the beginning of your learning comes from studying the features of the rainbow and making notes of your observations. Later, you can read more on rainbows and try to explain what you have seen.

The first thing to notice is what colors appear and how prominent each is—you will not always see the famous "seven colors of the rainbow," even if you can distinguish the least well-known color (indigo), between blue and violet. Red is on top, violet on the bottom. You may notice a couple of extra stripes of pale pink and green or blue below the lower edge of the regular rainbow. The cause of these *supernumerary arcs* is similar to that of the colors in oil splotches on roads after a rain, or of the coronas in clouds. How prominent certain colors in a rainbow are compared to each other, and what supernumerary arcs appear (if any are visible), depend largely on the size of the raindrops. If drops are fairly small, red is not visible and any arcs will be pale and colorless. The truly tiny droplets of mist or fog produce an entirely colorless bow. Dewdrops are big enough to make a colorful bow—on the ground!

Two other rainbow features to look for are a secondary rainbow and greater sky brightness beneath the main (or "primary") rainbow than above it. A *secondary rainbow* is not nearly as rare as many people think. It appears about 51° from the antisolar point (thus above the primary rainbow). It is about twice as wide as the primary and has the order of colors reversed (in the secondary, violet is the top color, red the bottom color).

2. Polarization of the Rainbow. *Observe and photograph whether the light from a rainbow is polarized.*

Do you or anyone you know have sunglasses that are polarizing? (Whether they are or not will often be mentioned on them or the tag that comes with them when bought.) Have a pair of sunglasses ready for when a rainbow appears and you can test whether the light from a rainbow is strongly polarized or not. If a rainbow's light is polarized, then the rainbow should be prominent with the sunglasses held one way, and weak or invisible with the glasses held at a 90° angle to the first way (say, vertically rather than horizontally).

Another experiment to test the polarization of light in the rainbow—one whose results you can show to others—is to photograph the rainbow with and without a polarizing filter. (Such filters, which screw onto the lens of a 35mm camera, are quite inexpensive.)

What other changes in the landscape and sky can you see with polarizing sunglasses? Do some reading on the polarization of light and what it is.

3. Halo Phenomena. *Observe different kinds of halo phenomena, sketching them and noting how often they occur.*

Halo phenomena are various circles, arcs, columns, and patches of light—some with brilliant colors—that are caused by reflection and sometimes refraction of sunlight in ice crystals. The ice crystals are usually found floating high up in the thin, feathery cirrus clouds we can see at any time of year (5 miles [8 km] up, it is cold enough for ice crystals even in summer).

The most famous halo phenomenon is probably the "ring around the moon," but a similar ring around the sun (and other daytime halo phenomena) can be more prominent and far more colorful, because the sun is much brighter. The technical name is the *22° halo*, because this circle has a radius of 22° (a bit more than two fist-widths at arm's length). Why is the 22° lunar halo more famous than the solar? Mostly because few people ever look in the general direction of the blazing sun. Actually, however, to see most halo phenomena when they occur, you don't have to look very close to the danger-ously bright sun (**Never stare right at the sun**—you could be blinded!).

Figure 4-1 shows where several of the most common halo phenomena occur and what shape they take. In reality, one tricky factor is that some of these halo effects change their shape and their position relative to the sun, somewhat depending on how high up the sun is. The *parhelia* (or "mock suns" or "sun dogs") are rarely seen when the sun is very high, and are right on the

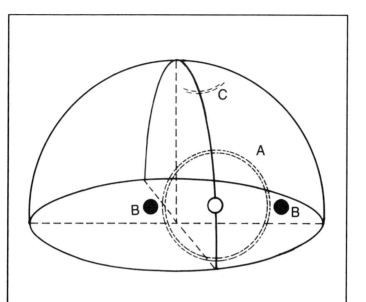

Figure 4-1. Where to look for some common halo phenomena when the sun is moderately low in the sky. At position A is the 22° halo. The parhelia (also known as mock suns and sun dogs) can be found at position B, and the circumzenithal arc at position C.

22° halo when the sun is rising and setting. The *circumzenithal arc*—which looks like a small, upside-down rainbow (lovely!)—is only visible when the sun is fairly low in the sky. And here's another important point: you may see only one or two of these halo phenomena at one time, or only part of one (the parhelia—or a single one, a parhelion—may occur without any trace of the 22° halo, or only part of the halo may be visible).

The most common halo phenomena of all are the 22° halo and the parhelia. Both the halo and the parhelia may show red on their parts towards the sun, other spectrum colors working out to blue on the edge farthest from the sun. Another fairly common halo phenomenon, one not shown on our diagram, is a *sun pillar*. This appears as a column of light extending straight up (less often, straight down) from the sun when the sun is either low in the sky or even a little below the horizon. The making of the pillar by the floating ice crystals does not involve refraction, so there are no spectrum colors but the pillar does take on the yellow, orange, or pink of the low sun that causes it.

How often can you see some kind of halo phenomenon? Depending on your climate and weather, seeing one kind or another several times each week is quite possible. Make a careful count of how many of each kind you do see over the course of weeks or months. What weather patterns seem to favor them? Be sure to sketch (or photograph) what each looked like and note how far from the sun it was and how high above the horizon the sun was (use your fist—see Figure 3-1—for these angular measurements).

4. Halos as Weather Predictors. *Study whether a 22° halo around the sun or moon is a good predictor of rain.*

A famous piece of weather lore says, "Ring around the moon means rain soon." The cirrus clouds that produce the ring around the moon and sun—the 22° halo—may precede a large storm system with widespread rain, proving the saying true. But how often does this happen? Keep a record of when you see at least a part of a 22° halo around the sun or moon and how many hours or days later you get rain. (You should also find out from the local TV weather report what kind of weather system caused the rain: a cold front? a warm front? a local thundershower on a hot day?)

5. Coronas and Iridescent Clouds. *Observe coronas and iridescent clouds around the moon and sun, noting what*

*kinds of clouds are best for them and how far from the moon
or sun they extend.*

Coronas are disks and rings of color right around the moon and sun—far smaller (closer to the moon and sun) than halos. You're most likely to see patches of corona color on clouds as they pass the moon when it is bright. You will notice that the lovely pastel pinks and blues or greens always appear on a cloud when it reaches the same position near the moon. If there is enough cloud around the moon, you may get to see around the moon an entire disk of blue-green with an outside border of red. An entire separate cloud which gets these colors farther, sometimes much farther, from the moon or sun in the sky is called an *iridescent cloud.*

Coronas are usually caused by tiny cloud droplets of water (more rarely, by special ice crystals called ice needles). These droplets are similar in size to the waves which make up light (we sometimes talk as if light were "rays," or as if it were particles called "photons," but that is another story). The little droplets act to block light of certain color from some places, and reinforce it in others. And so we get blue-green (short wavelengths of light) near the moon, and red (long wavelengths of light) farther out. (This corona pattern of blue or green with red outside of it may be repeated several times— though dimmer—the farther from the moon our gaze takes us: blue-green, red; blue-green, red; blue-green, red.)

Coronas are surprisingly common, occurring in many kinds of moderately thick clouds with the moon and with almost all kinds of clouds that the sun can be glimpsed through. Observing the colors near the blinding sun can be difficult and dangerous. Instead, look at the coronas and iridescent clouds around the sun in its reflection in a puddle of still water, or a car windshield.

Keep notes of when you see coronas and iridescent clouds, including how large the corona was (angular measure—use your fist or finger at arm's length, or compare with the $\frac{1}{2}°$-wide disk of the moon itself). Also try to determine what kind of cloud produced a given display. The best clouds for these phenomena are altocumulus lenticularis—lens-shaped "wave clouds" which you can read more about in a good book on weather.

SUNSETS AND TWILIGHTS

6. Low-Sun Phenomena. *Watch each day as the sun gets low to see how red and flattened it becomes, whether there are any other distortions of its shape as it sets, and whether you can glimpse the "green flash."*

When the sun is low in the sky, it shines through a longer pathway of our atmosphere. This dims the sun a lot, but you must still be careful and not look at the sun unless it is enormously dimmed, very near the horizon. Why does the low sun look red? All the wavelengths of light (colors) except the long wavelengths (red) get mostly absorbed or scattered by the journey through the greater thickness of atmosphere low in the sky.

The thicker air down low also refracts (bends) our image of the lower part of the sun up more than it does the upper edge, so the sun seems flattened (smaller in the vertical dimension than in the horizontal one). Note, sketch, or photograph how reddened and flattened the sun gets on various nights. See how humidity and air pollution affect the sun's reddening. See how a large difference between air and ground temperature (or air and water temperature, if you watch the sunset over a large lake, bay, or ocean) will affect how flattened the sun gets—and what other strange distortions of shape it may cause.

Finally, as the last piece of sun disappears below the horizon, always look in case that last piece suddenly changes color to green, offering you the marvel of the *green flash*. If you live in some climates (say, in California, looking out over the Pacific), you may see some version of the green flash many times a year. In most places, though, the green flash is quite rare. You have a chance of seeing it if the air is quite clear and fewer of the blue and green wavelengths of sunlight are scattered out. As the sun sets, the image of the sun in green light is refracted slightly more, slightly higher than the image of the sun in red light. Thus, the top edge of the sun becomes predominantly green and can be seen as such for just a second after the reddish rest of the sun has set. Note air and water (or ground) temperature and humidity whenever you manage to see the green flash.

7. **Twilight Glows.** *Look for the various twilight glows, seeing how prominent each is, how high each extends, how long after sunset each lasts.*

Twilight is the period between sunset and night (or night and sunrise), when the sun has disappeared below the horizon as seen from our view at ground level but still lights up the atmosphere miles above us to the west at dusk (east at dawn). These twilights usually only become truly spectacular in the months and years after a major volcanic eruption somewhere in the world has produced a worldwide haze of ash or sulfuric acid droplets high in the atmosphere. But since 1980 that situation—volcanic haze, spectacular twilights—has been in effect more often than not.

The first thing to look for from a *volcanic twilight* is a thick band of white or gold light becoming orange or red along the west horizon at or soon after sunset. You will not see much color unless the atmosphere is mostly cloud-free for hundreds of miles west (or, rather, sunward) of you (check the satellite photo on TV weather to see when this is so). Next comes the most stunning part of a volcanic twilight: the appearance of the *purple light* (also called "secondary glow"). Partway up the western sky a huge patch of usually more pink than purple radiance appears and strengthens. This usually starts about twenty minutes after sunset, but the timing can vary for several reasons. Note the time when the purple light appears, when it is strongest, when the last colorful trace of it has set. Measure how many degrees high the top of the purple light is at various times. The higher that its top edge is at a given time after sunset, the higher in the atmosphere the haze of volcanic material must lie in order to be still catching the sunlight.

For a few years after a really mighty eruption (El Chichon volcano in Mexico in 1982, Pinatubo volcano of the Philippines in 1991), we even get to see some nights when a mysterious *second purple light* appears where the first one did in the western sky after the sinking first purple light disappears! This second purple light usually is more purple than the first—and its last traces (sometimes turned ruby red) may glow in the west even until the rest of the sky fills up with stars.

LIGHT POLLUTION

8. Identifying Light Pollution. *Locate light pollution glows in the sky in various directions from where you live or observe, and try to determine what their source is.*

What is the greatest practical problem facing today's amateur and professional astronomer? It is *light pollution,* civilization's excessive and misdirected outdoor lighting. As much as several billion dollars' worth of light goes off uselessly into space from the United States each year, mostly because of poorly shielded and otherwise poorly directed man-made lights.

The first project to teach you more about light pollution and what you can do about it involves identifying the major sources of light pollution surrounding you.

Just pick any evening when the moon is not up, preferably one that is fairly clear.

If you live in a fairly large city, the entire sky over you for miles around may be lit up with skyglow (the light escaping up to the sky from a city or other source). But are there directions in which the glow is more intense and your view of the stars more dimmed? Perhaps you are seeing the downtown shopping district, a car dealership, or a shopping mall. Some malls and city street-lighting systems are much better than others, saving us all energy and money and actually giving us better visibility by using properly shielded lighting. Try to learn what parts of town or what businesses are producing the most light pollution.

If you live or observe from out in the country, you will still almost certainly be able to find some patches of skyglow coming up from several spots along your horizon. Figure out (with a compass or otherwise) what directions these glows lie in; then use a map to figure out which cities are causing which glows. You may be astonished at how far away the light pollution of a large, wasteful city can be seen.

9. Strength of City Skyglows: Size Versus Distance. *After comparing the strength of skyglows from different cities as seen from one or more observing sites, estimate which is more important in producing light pollution: the closeness of a city, or its population—and estimate how much more important the one is than the other.*

Scientists have worked out formulas to predict how much light pollution to expect from a city of a given population at a given distance. The formulas have produced surprising results. If you assume that the amount of light pollution from a typical city is roughly equivalent to its population (a city of 200,000 people would produce about twice as much light pollution as a city of 100,000), you are right. But if you assume that a city

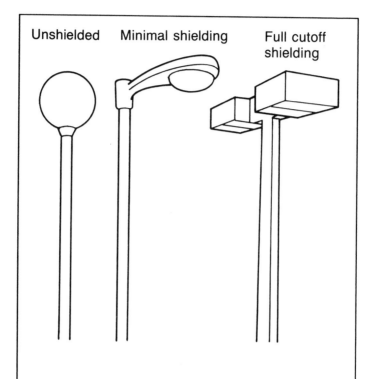

Figure 4-2. Different types of shielding for outdoor lighting. Unshielded is the most wasteful (i.e., sends off the most light into the sky), and full cutoff shielding the least wasteful.

with twice as many people (and twice as much light pollution) would have to be twice as far to affect your sky no more than the smaller city, you are wrong.

Is it worse to have a fairly small city close to you, or a tremendously larger one fairly far away? Go out on a moonless evening and find out for yourself. If you live at a suburban or rural location, you can study the sky-glows from various cities along your horizon. If you live in the midst of a fairly large city, you will have to get someone to drive you to a place miles outside of your city to survey where the light pollution glows from a number of cities lie.

Rate the strength of the different skyglows. How many degrees up is each noticeable? How many bright stars are almost lost from view in each glow? Now use a map with a list of city populations—any road map will probably do fine. Just measure the distance from your observing spot to each of the cities and then draw your conclusions—is distance or size of a city more important?

One final note: some cities are more wasteful of light than others. If the city is Atlantic City, New Jersey, with its casinos and associated lighting, you would find that the skyglow is much worse than suggested by the small figure for the resident population. On the other hand, a city with only half the light pollution you'd expect from its population is Tucson, Arizona, which has passed excellent laws against light pollution and uses money-saving practices and technology to reduce it (Figure 4-2). For lots more information on how Tucson has done it, and on light pollution in general, write to the International Dark-Sky Association, 3545 N. Stewart, Tucson, AZ 85716.

Exploring the Moon, the Sun, and Eclipses

Chapter 5

THE MOON

Lunar Phases, Motion, Size, Earthshine

1. The Moon's Phases. *Identify the moon's phases with the place and time of night the moon is visible and with the part of the moon's orbit it is in.*

The moon's phases are caused by different amounts of its Earthward-pointing face being lit by the sun at different parts of its orbit (Figure 5-1). Figure 5-2 shows this clearly. But in what parts of the sky and what parts of the night do we see the moon when it is at its different phases, at the various places in its orbit? Our first moon project helps clarify this matter.

First, check your calendar for when new moon occurs. New moon is the invisible phase when the moon is lost to view because it is setting with the sun and in any case pointing its night side toward us. So you know the new moon is low in the west at sunset (if you want a bit more proof, go out a few days later at sunset and locate the skinny crescent moon, still fairly low in the west).

The next step is to search ahead on your calendar and go out—again at sunset—to look for the first-quarter and full moon at sunset, and identify where they are. One word of warning: if the weather forecast a few days in advance predicts that the actual day of first-quarter

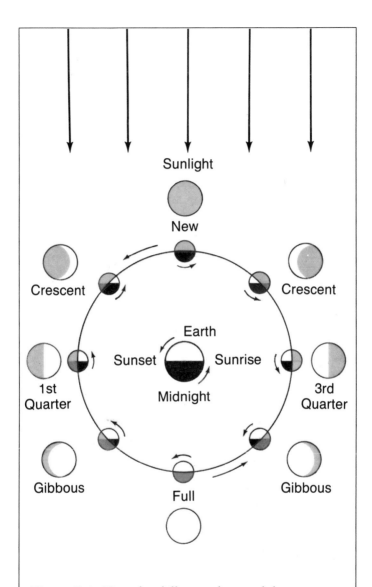

Figure 5-1. How the different phases of the moon are caused. The lined area is the side of the moon always pointed away from Earth, and dark and light areas indicate day and night sides of the moon at various times.

Figure 5-2. Photograph of the moon taken by
New Jersey amateur astronomer Tom Connelly

or full moon will not be clear, go out and look at the moon a day or two before these phases. (If you go out the day after full moon, you may have to wait until more than an hour after sunset before the moon even rises.) And for the full moon, add on a new observation: go out to see where the full moon (or moon a few days before full) is at sunrise, or a little before sunrise.

Next, a bit of a change. Pick a clear day near the date of last-quarter moon, but this time go out only at sunrise (the last-quarter moon is not up in the sky at sunset). Where is the last-quarter moon at the time the sun comes up? (By the way, you may enjoy watching this moon in the blue sky as the morning progresses— have you ever noticed the moon in the daytime sky before?)

Now comes the final stage in this monthlong project. Go out on the next day of new moon at sunrise (even if it is cloudy, you will know the sun is coming up). Imagine the moon rising with the sun in the east and setting with the sun in the west that day, bringing us back to the starting point of this project.

Even if a cloudy week causes you to miss one of these observations, you may be able to understand the pattern of where and when each phase—new moon, first quarter, full moon, last quarter, and new moon again— appears. Compare your observations with our diagram to see if you can make sense of why each of these phases appears where it does at sunset or sunrise.

2. The Moon's Night-to-Night Motion. *Observe the moon on a series of nights to see how its position in the sky changes during the course of an evening and from one night to the next, noting also how its time of setting or rising changes.*

Our goal in this project is to learn to distinguish between the apparent motion of the moon and its true, orbital motion.

On a series of nights starting a few nights after new moon, locate and note the moon's position in relation to bright background stars around it and also when the moon sets each night. Do the same on a series of nights soon after full moon, except note when the moon rises each night.

Which way (eastward or westward) does the moon appear to move as it heads towards setting, or heads away from its rising? This rapid motion during the night is not really the moon's. It is caused by our Earth's rotation: the Earth's carrying us rapidly in one direction makes it look like the moon is traveling the opposite way across our sky.

Which way (eastward or westward) does the moon appear to be heading when you compare its position from one night to the next night? This time, the motion you are detecting (or inferring from the moon's change of position) is its true orbital motion. If you don't believe that the moon is moving very slowly (about one of its own diameters per hour) in this direction, check during the length of an entire evening how its position changes in relation to a bright background star too distant to show any motion of its own.

3. The Moon's Size and the Moon Illusion. *See how small a cardboard disk held at arm's length has to be to just cover the disk of the moon when the moon is both low and high. Then try to experiment to see what factors produce the illusion that the moon is bigger when low in the sky.*

The moon is not just tremendously brighter than any other object in the night sky; it is the only really bright object which shows considerable size. These are no doubt the main reasons why we tend to overestimate how big the moon is in the sky.

Some people think it would take a coin at least as

large as a quarter held at arm's length to cover the moon. They're wrong. Preferably when the moon is nearly full, try a series of cardboard disks of various sizes you have cut out to see which one covers the moon exactly when you hold it at arm's length. This experiment is guaranteed to amaze you—far more if you do it and see it for yourself than if someone tells you the answer.

After you've done it, you're ready for the more challenging and useful part of our project: trying to figure out what produces the moon illusion, the illusion that the moon is bigger when it is down near the horizon. All of us at one time or other have been awed by a rising or setting moon seemingly as big as a grapefruit. But use your cardboard disk. You will find that the seemingly hugest rising moon is still covered by your tiny cardboard disk, and gets no smaller when high in the sky. (In fact, the moon gets very slightly bigger when high in the sky because the Earth has turned us to a point under the moon and therefore several thousand miles closer to it.)

What causes the moon illusion? Is it that a low moon looks huge because it is beside distant and therefore tiny-looking objects in our landscape? Try to test this by looking at the low moon through a tube that isolates it from comparison objects. If it still looks large, then there must be more to the moon illusion. Another theory is that the direction of our gaze in relation to our body has an effect. Lean forward so that you have to cast your eyes up in relation to your body to see the moon: does the moon then look smaller?

Apparently, whatever makes us perceive the horizon as being farther will make the moon look correspondingly bigger. But what factors make us feel the horizon is farther? Judge on a series of nights before and after full moon (early autumn is the best time, for several reasons) how dramatic the moon illusion is as the moon comes up and which of these factors is in effect each night: twilight or daylight; general cloudiness; individual clouds; distant objects in the landscape.

4. Earthshine. *Observe earthshine on the moon, rating its strength and checking on whether this corresponds with how much cloudiness there is on the daytime side of the Earth at the time of your observation.*

Have you ever seen the crescent moon and then noticed that the supposedly dark part of the moon is also lit, though far less brightly than the crescent part? The prominence of this phenomenon varies greatly from night to night and month to month. The phenomenon is called *earthshine* and it literally is the light of a nearly "full" Earth shining on the night side of the moon.

The larger the lunar phase gets, the more the sunlit part of the moon overwhelms the earthshine. (Also, the larger the moon's phase is as seen from Earth, the smaller the Earth's phase gets as seen from the moon, resulting in less earthshine.) But why is it that some months the earthshine at a certain phase—say, three days after new moon—is much brighter than it is at that same phase other months? The answer must be that sometimes the daytime side of Earth shining on the moon has more clouds on it and therefore reflects more light onto the moon.

It's fun and fascinating to observe earthshine and rate it—say on a 1 to 10 scale from the weakest to the strongest you've ever seen. But even more interesting is testing this theory about the cloudy Earth. If you live in the United States or southern Canada the part of the Earth experiencing daytime while you watch the crescent moon after sunset is mostly the Pacific Ocean. Some TV weather reports do show satellite photos of some of the Pacific (your best bet for the most extensive coverage of the Pacific would likely be cable TV's Weather

Channel). Can you demonstrate a correspondence be-tween your observations of a strong earthshine and a cloudy Pacific? Just think how marvelous it would be to judge what the weather was like halfway around the world by looking at the moon!

Lunar Features • Who hasn't gasped with astonish-ment and delight when getting a first look at the moon through a telescope—or even a thousandth look? Hundreds of lunar features are visible in chisel-sharp perfection through a pair of binoculars, perhaps a few million through a medium-size amateur telescope. And the appearance of these plains, craters, mountains, val-leys, and other mysterious parts of the moon's landscape changes dramatically from night to night, even hour to hour, as the angle of sunlight falling on them changes.

In this series of projects, Projects 5 through 7, you will observe outstanding examples of a variety of lunar features with binoculars or a telescope. These projects are intended to be just a first survey of the moon. Their goal is to have you sample the major kinds of lunar features. Still, you could make a whole project out of observing and sketching any one of the individual cra-ters or other features (especially if you sketched it dur-ing the whole course of time it is illuminated during a month—as I suggest in an upcoming project).

One reminder is useful: remember that most features on the moon are more clearly seen when they are near the terminator, the line separating light from dark (day from night) on the moon. As the moon progresses from a waxing (thickening) crescent in the evening to first quarter and on to full in two weeks, we see the termi-nator move across the entire face of the moon. An as-tronaut on the moon would experience sunrise as this terminator reached him or her before full moon. After full moon, the terminator is the sunset line, again creeping across the moon's face right to left (as seen from Earth's northern hemisphere), but this time bringing nighttime to each location.

Why are most features seen more clearly at the terminator? Think of it this way. If you were an astronaut at the terminator, the sun would be low in the sky, and the long shadows the features cast would make every tiny bump or ditch in the landscape stand out in sharp detail. On the other hand, when the sun hangs high over a crater or mountain range, the shadows are slight and details are washed out by the sunlight that almost evenly illuminates everything. The sunlight shining almost straight back to us from the full moon is so bright it bothers our eyes in a medium-size telescope at low magnification. A full moon is not just twice but about a dozen times brighter than a half moon, because the full moon contains virtually no shadow.

The only one of the following features which is not most sharply seen within a night or two of when the sunlight has just started hitting it are the rays. These are believed to be long streaks of more reflective dust thrown out from some of the younger craters on the moon when they were made by meteorite impacts. They have no appreciable height or depth and therefore don't cast shadows. They are seen well only when the high sun shines down on them, making them light up.

In order to find the following features, use a simplified moon map. Once you learn some of these most spectacular features, you'll be ready to use a more detailed map and start finding out what all those other captivating lunar sights are!

5. Maria, or Lunar "Seas." *Using binoculars or a telescope, observe and sketch maria (singular, mare).*

These "seas" on the moon are not really oceans, of course (the moon is too small to have enough gravity to hold water or air). They are vast gray plains of hardened lava—lava which flowed in to fill the huge scars caused by the impacts of asteroid-size bodies in the crowded, wild days of the early solar system. Most of the maria are approximately 4 billion years old. The maria are so large and prominent that many of them can be seen with the naked eye—they are the familiar dark markings on the moon.

Which mare is the most interesting to look at in binoculars or telescope? Perhaps the most beautiful of all is one of the least ancient, the Mare Imbrium ("Sea of Dreams"). This large mare is almost surrounded by four major mountain ranges, and at one edge of it is the lovely Sinus Iridum ("Bay of Rainbows"). The terminator crosses Mare Imbrium in the days just after first quarter, just before last quarter. Try also to see and sketch the other maria, including Oceanus Procellarum ("Ocean of Storms"), the biggest but one of the least well formed of the maria.

6. Craters. *Observe and sketch craters, and note "foreshortening" and "libration."*

Even the largest craters look rather small in binoculars but in a telescope they of course dominate almost every view of the moon. They range in size from well over a hundred miles (160 km) across to a mile (1.6 km) wide (about the smallest a medium-size amateur telescope will show) and on down to the tiniest pittings of the surface (as the Apollo astronauts found out when they walked on the moon). The craters are caused by meteorite impacts, but they are far more like shallow dishes than deep bowls or holes. True, the distance from the rim to the bottom of some craters is several miles—but these craters are dozens of miles across. Note that in many craters a spectacular central mountain mass was thrown up by the meteorite impact.

When choosing which craters to observe, we are faced with, as the saying goes, "an embarrassment of riches." Which wondrous sight should we study first? The crater Copernicus would get many lunar observers' votes for first: it has few rivals in prominence, perfection of form, complexity (study the details of the triple mountain mass inside it carefully).

Not far from Copernicus is the smaller but similarly splendid Kepler and the most brilliant crater on the moon, Aristarchus. Farther toward the "west" edge of the moon (lunar west, which is the side facing east in our sky) is the darkest feature, the crater Grimaldi. Near the northern edge, or "limb," of the moon, not far north of Mare Imbrium, is another dark and well-formed crater—Plato.

But speaking of form: do you notice that Plato is a far more elongated circle—really an ellipse—than Copernicus and many other craters are? Actually Plato shares this appearance with all craters that appear fairly near the edge of the moon as seen from Earth. If you could fly directly over Plato in a spacecraft you would find it just about as circular as Copernicus or any crater. The reason it and all the other craters (indeed all the lunar features) near the limb look "foreshortened"—compressed in one dimension—is merely the sideways angle at which we behold them. A coin in the palm of your hand looks circular if you look straight down on it, but pick it up and start tilting it more toward a sideways view and you'll see that its apparent shape becomes an oval or ellipse, and finally when seen from the side a mere line.

By the way, after you've observed the moon closely for a few months you'll notice that sometimes the features near a certain limb of the moon—west, southwest, northeast, whatever—appear distinctly more or distinctly less foreshortened than usual. This is caused by the fact that the Earthward-pointing face of the moon is sometimes tilted a bit more up, down, or to either side. This tilting, called *libration,* is mostly caused by a complexity of the moon's orbital motion that gives us a slightly different vantage point on it. There is one effect of libration that is spectacularly noticeable to the naked eye: the lovely isolated Mare Crisium sometimes appears much closer to the upper right edge of the moon, and at such times far more foreshortened (almost into a line as seen with the naked eye).

What other craters are good subjects for our project? About three days after new moon, the north-south line of craters called Langrenus, Vendelinus, and Petavius is beautiful in telescopes, detectable in good binoculars. About five days after new moon, the spectacular Theophilus and its neighbors Cyrillus and Catharina are well placed for viewing. And for several days around first quarter (or last quarter) you can get superb views of the numerous craters near the moon's central meridian: Ptolemaeus, Alphonsus, Arzachel, Walter, and, farther south, Tycho, Maginus, and the giant Clavius.

7. Other Lunar Features. *Observe and sketch other kinds of lunar features—mountain ranges and mountains, rays, valleys, rills, and more.*

There's far more to the lunar landscape than its many huge maria and countless craters. For one thing, there are the mountain ranges which border some of the maria—the moon's mightiest range is the Apennines, stretching for 600 miles (965 km) and with peaks as high as 18,000 feet (5,500 m). Look for it in the few days after first quarter when it can even make a bump on the terminator visible to the naked eye. Other mountain ranges are notable for standing out by themselves on one of the otherwise flat maria—note the Straight Range on Mare Imbrium. Isolated mountains and their shadows are also prominent: not far from the Straight Range are the individual peaks Pico and Piton, spectacular at a fairly high magnification just after first quarter.

The rays some craters have is dramatic around full moon. The crowning example is the ray system of Tycho. Binoculars suffice to show some of its rays, one of which may extend for over 1,000 miles (1,600 km)! Kepler has a lesser but also impressive ray system.

Valleys and narrow, winding ravines called rills are often tricky to see unless you look when the terminator is near and they stand out from the surrounding bright landscape because their depths are still in darkness. The 80-mile-long (130 km) Alpine Valley is a beautiful split through the Alps Mountains of the moon. Although it is called a valley, Schroter's Valley is narrower and more winding, and is therefore classified as a rill. Look for it coming out of the crater Herodotus, which is near bright Aristarchus.

For a challenge, look for a unique and beautiful lunar feature called the Straight Wall. A few days after first quarter it appears as a dark line; around full moon it disappears; then, around last quarter, it shines out as a brilliant line! What is it? The Straight Wall is a fairly steep cliff (technically, a "fault") which is over 1,000 feet (300 m) tall and runs for about 75 miles (120 km). The cliff faces lunar west and thus is brightly lit by sunset on the moon around last quarter.

COPERNICUS, AND LUNAR LANDING SITES

8. Studying a Crater. *With a telescope, observe and sketch the appearance of the crater Copernicus, or another lunar feature of your choice, from the time it first is lit until it last is lit during the month.*

The angle of sunlight on craters and other lunar features makes a tremendous difference as to what appearance they present to us. Some worn, very shallow craters are completely lost from view when the sun gets too high over them. That is not the case with Copernicus. Its topography (ups and downs of landscape) is best seen when it is near the terminator, but its patches and rays of reflective dust light up magnificently near full moon. So there is something special—and different—to see in it every night it is illuminated.

As you perform this project, you will notice that on some nights images on the moon are not as sharp as on others. (This is especially noticeable as you increase your magnification.) The reason? The Earth's atmosphere above you is less steady on some nights and does not permit very sharp views—in other words, there is bad "seeing."

9. Lunar Landing Sites. *With a telescope, observe and sketch the regions in which Apollo astronauts landed and walked on the moon in the period from 1969 to 1972.*

A generation has passed since men walked on the moon. But you can study those glorious missions and look at the areas on the moon that these explorers visited. You will only see the larger features in the vicinities of where they landed, walked, collected moon rocks. But your observations will still be thrilling.

The accompanying map (Figure 5-3) shows you where to look. Of course, your observations will mean something to you only if you also read about the details of the missions. What happened in the years preceding the Apollo program that built up to it? What spacecraft were used? What were the different stages of each flight and visit? Who were the astronauts that went? What did these astronauts do while on the moon? These are some of the questions you can find answers to.

Copies of the photos the astronauts took could be displayed with the sketches of your observations for a fine science fair project. But I think you might enjoy making these observations and sketches even if you don't use them for a science fair!

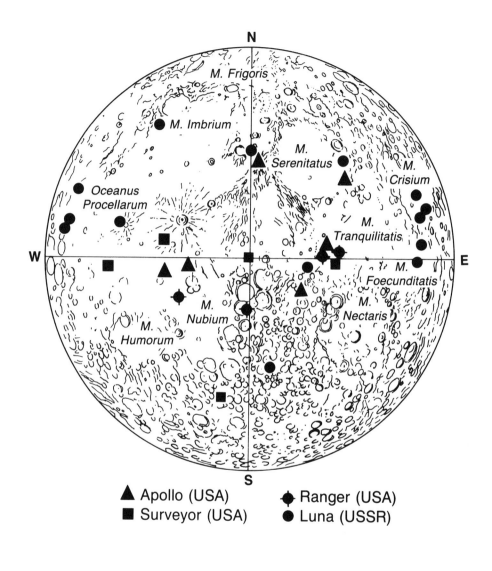

Figure 5-3. Map of the moon showing where manned and unmanned spacecraft landed

10. The Sun and Sunspots. *Observe the sun and count sunspots safely by using the telescopic projection method—with the guidance of a knowledgeable adult.*

Imagine somehow snatching a big, sunspot-speckled image of the sun from the midst of its blinding glare. The surface of the sun is literally blinding—you could permanently lose some or all of your eyesight if you try to look right at it without proper protection. **Never observe the sun directly without using a proper filter.** I even advise beginners not to use the filters provided with some inexpensive telescopes because many of these filters are not well made and could be dangerous. The best way to get a beautiful image of the sun and count sunspots is to use *solar projection.*

Even projection requires caution. Read these instructions carefully with a knowledgeable adult and have that adult on hand to supervise you. Make certain that anyone who is unaware of the danger does not get near or in line with the eyepiece of the telescope.

The first step in projection is to put the sun at your back and get it into your telescope without ever looking through the telescope (Figure 5-4). **(Never look through the telescope at the sun!)** You can do this by adjusting the telescope until its tube casts the smallest possible shadow. When it does, the sun should be shining directly into your telescope.

Now all you need is some kind of screen—preferably mounted, but even a hand-held piece of cardboard is adequate. (Be careful where you put your fingers, though; there is a point where a lot of heat is focused.) You should see a very bright circle or area of light on your screen. In order to turn it into a sharp image of the sun adjust the distance of the screen from the eyepiece of the telescope (or focus the eyepiece). Even if you are

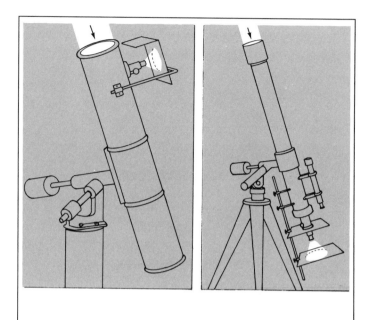

Figure 5-4. Setups for solar projection with a reflecting telescope (left) and a refracting telescope (right)

using a quite small telescope there is a good chance you will see a few sunspots, probably in groups.

Observe where sunspots are on the sun on a number of days in a row. You will find that they are moving across the face of the sun—or, rather, that the sun is rotating! The sun rotates at different rates at different latitudes, but you can get a rough idea of how long one full rotation takes by timing how long it takes for a sunspot group to go from one edge of the sun to the other.

An even more fascinating thing about sunspots is that their numbers and position on the sun are indicators of the mysterious eleven-year cycle of solar activity.

This cycle, which is not always exactly eleven years, goes from one minimum of solar activity to the next minimum. In between, the solar maximum is a time of many solar flares (eruptions of atomic particles from the sun which enrich the usual particle flow, the *solar wind*, and may cause those colorful, moving patterns of radiance called the *northern lights*, or the *aurora borealis*, in Earth's upper atmosphere with the help of Earth's magnetic field). Solar maximum is also a time of most plentiful sunspots. The last solar maximum was in 1989, the next solar minimum may occur around 1996 or 1997. But even around solar minimum you can usually find a few sunspots.

Exactly what causes sunspots is a mystery although they are certainly associated with the sun's powerful magnetic field. They often occur in pairs. How does a sunspot or a sunspot group change during the course of a few days? Be sure to count not just how many spots but how many groups you see. How many of the spots are all dark (called an *umbra*)? How many have a lighter outer *penumbra* (these terms are used in regard to shadows in eclipses, too, remember).

Think of the fact that some of these spots are immensely larger than the Earth—and that although cooler than the surrounding surface of the sun they are still thousands of degrees hot and would shine brightly if they were not overwhelmed by the even more radiant and hot surface surrounding them.

ECLIPSES

11. Eclipses of the Moon. *Study the progress of the Earth's shadow across the moon during partial eclipse; note colors and rate the darkness of the moon on the Danjon scale during total eclipse.*

An eclipse of the moon is a long, fascinating show that is always filled with surprises. Each one is different.

In fact, nobody can predict exactly how dark the moon will get or exactly what colors will appear on its face at a particular eclipse.

You may be lucky enough to get to witness a lunar eclipse this year (see Appendix 5 for a list of when and where they do occur in the 1990s). If you do see one, your observations will make for an interesting science fair project—especially if the eclipse is total.

Of course, not all lunar eclipses are total.

In a penumbral lunar eclipse the moon passes through only the penumbra, the less dark, outer part of Earth's shadow. Only if it passes more than halfway into the penumbra will you see even the slightest shading on the edge of the moon (the edge farthest into the shadow). At such an eclipse, note what time you are first sure that you see the subtle darkening and what time you are last sure you see it.

In a partial lunar eclipse the moon passes into the umbra, the darker, inner part of Earth's shadow, but only part of the moon does so. The umbra is plainly visible to the naked eye within a few minutes after it touches the lunar surface, and this is immediately excit-ing when you stop and think about what you are seeing. That "bite" of darkness taken out of the moon is the shadow of the very planet you stand upon. And notice the shape of the shadow. It has a curved edge: you are seeing direct evidence that the Earth is round.

What else can you see during a partial eclipse of the moon? You can watch the dramatic movement of the shadow across each lunar mare with the naked eye, and across craters, mountains, and other lunar features with binoculars or telescope. Unless you are in a big city (where bright lights always overwhelm the stars), you can also watch more and more stars come out as less and less of the moon remains outside the umbra.

A total eclipse of the moon is tremendously more exciting and beautiful than a penumbral lunar eclipse or partial lunar eclipse. At each total eclipse, we get to see the moon first go into the penumbra (as in a penumbral eclipse), then go partway into the umbra (as in a partial eclipse). But the moon continues deeper into the umbra—until at last it is totally covered.

That is the time for real surprises, because we can never be sure exactly how dark the moon will get. Many people think that the moon is supposed to get completely dark when it is totally eclipsed. Actually, that rarely happens. In most cases, the moon, though greatly dimmed, shines with a reddish (sometimes more orange or pink) light. What we are seeing is the reddened light of all Earth's current sunrises and sunsets bent by our atmosphere into Earth's shadow and onto the moon. An astronaut on the moon would see the sun hidden and a ring of red light around the huge dark form of the Earth.

Just how dark the moon gets, just what shade of color it turns, depends on how much cloudiness and haze there is at places along the sunrise-sunset line (the terminator) on Earth. The really dark lunar eclipses occur when even the usually clear atmosphere above ordinary clouds is filled with the haze from a recent great volcanic eruption. There were very dark total eclipses of the moon in 1982 after the eruption of the El Chichon volcano in Mexico and in 1992 after the eruption of Mt. Pinatubo in the Philippines.

You can rate the darkness and overall color of the eclipse by using the *Danjon scale* (Table 2). In some unusual eclipses you may find the darkness of the moon deserves one rating early in the eclipse and another rating later.

And don't forget that you may see other colors here and there on the moon during the lunar eclipse, both with the naked eye and with binoculars or telescope. Sometimes the edge of the umbra has beautiful colors. I have seen shades of red, blue, green, yellow, brown,

Table 2 Danjon's Brightness Scale
for Total Lunar Eclipses

0 Very dark eclipse; moon hardly visible, especially near mid-totality

1 Dark eclipse; gray to brown coloring; details on the disk hardly discernible

2 Dark red or rust-colored eclipse with dark area in the center of shadow, the edge brighter

3 Brick-red eclipse, the shadow often bordered with a brighter yellow edge

4 Orange or copper-colored, very bright eclipse with bright bluish edge

---

gray, silver, even purple in total eclipses of the moon. What will you see, and sketch?

12. Eclipses of the Sun. *Use shade 14 welder's glass with your naked eye or the projection method with binoculars, telescope, or pinhole and follow the changing appearance of a partial solar eclipse or annular eclipse; note the change in the landscape's illumination, the sky's brightness and color, and the behavior of animals during a partial eclipse.*

Never look at a solar eclipse directly without proper eye protection (unless it is the total part of a total eclipse). An eclipse of the sun can be observed well by using the projection method of solar observation described in Figure 5-4. As a matter of fact, whereas you had to use the magnification of binoculars or telescope to be sure to see sunspots in our earlier project, a solar eclipse also can be viewed by projection with nothing more than a pinhole in a piece of cardboard—or even with the little gaps between leaves that produce bright circles and ellipses in the shade of a tree. Those circles and ellipses are actual images of the sun! And during a solar eclipse you can see a "bite" taken out of every one of them.

The "bite" is, of course, the dark form of the moon moving in front of the sun. And you can make a tiny but sharp image of that sun-with-a-bite-out-of-it with a piece of cardboard. Make a pinhole in the cardboard and, never looking directly at the sun (in fact, turning your back to the sun), position the cardboard so that sunlight shines straight through it. In the midst of its shadow on the ground (or on another piece of cardboard you use as a screen), you will see the little image of the sun. Adjust the distance between pinhole and screen until you get a sharp image. Experiment with making the pinhole bigger. What happens?

There is a kind of filter you can purchase for little money that is absolutely safe to use with your unaided eye. (*Note:* **Never use this filter with binoculars or telescope**—they have so much light-gathering power that the filter wouldn't be sufficient to protect you.) What is this filter? It is shade 14 welder's glass. Don't use a lower-number shade or your eyes will not be adequately protected (remember, it is the invisible ultraviolet light that is most dangerous—and you would not feel it burning the retinas of your eyes until perhaps you were blinded). A piece of shade 14 welder's glass large enough to look through will cost you about $2 or less from a welding supply company in your area. Just remember to ask for a piece many days or weeks before an eclipse: many welding supply stores don't carry this very dark glass in stock, and so must order it for you.

The image of the sun will look green through this welder's glass, but you will be able to see its changing shape during the eclipse very well.

There's more to solar eclipses than the change in the sun's appearance, though. Try noticing (and photographing) the alterations in the brightness (and color)

Figure 5-5. Artist's rendering of a total eclipse of the sun, showing the sun's gently glowing outer atmosphere, the corona

of the landscape and sky. These may not become noticeable unless the moon moves at least a third of the way across the sun. If you observe a large partial or annular eclipse, the changes will be striking, quite unlike anything you've ever seen before. You may see birds return to their roosts for the night and other animals act strange. You may spot Venus as it becomes visible to the naked eye in the darkening sky.

If you think a total eclipse of the moon is very beautiful, wait until you see a total eclipse of the sun (Figure 5-5). In order to see one, you will almost certainly have to travel somewhere else in the world, for while a partial solar eclipse is visible over large regions of the Earth, total solar eclipses are seen only from narrow bands of the Earth. I can't begin to tell you all the marvels you will see and experience and all the experiments you can try during a total eclipse of the sun. My advice is to learn about total solar eclipses—and keep in mind the idea of taking a vacation and traveling somewhere to see one in the years ahead. Some people have called a total solar eclipse the most awesome event in all of nature.

Exploring Meteors, Comets, and the Planets

Chapter 6

METEORS AND COMETS

1. Meteors. *Watch for meteors from a reasonably dark suburban or country location and record their brightness, colors, trails, and other properties.*

Meteors are those thrilling streaks of light which are sometimes called "shooting stars" or "falling stars." They are actually pieces of space rock or iron that have entered our atmosphere at stupendous speeds and therefore burn up from friction even with the incredibly thin air 50 or more miles (80 km) above us. Most people have seen none, one, or only a few meteors in their lives. But there are ways to increase your chances greatly—even ways to see dozens of meteors in a single hour.

Your first project is just to see—and describe—a few meteors. Your chances of seeing one are quite good if you stand or sit out for a while on any clear, moonless night far from city lights. Another piece of advice is to look in the second half of the night if possible. That is when meteors are more numerous and brighter, though usually also faster.

What features of meteors do you look for? Brightness is certainly one. How does the meteor compare in brightness to various stars? Is it one of those relatively rare meteors that are brighter than even the planet Venus and are called *fireballs?* Meteors also come in many colors: blue, green, red, even orange and pink may be seen, though many meteors are not bright enough to show any color at all. How far across the sky does your meteor travel, how long does it last, how fast is it (though all meteors are fast, you'll notice some are much faster than others)? From what point among the constellations (or at least what direction) does it seem to come? To what point does it seem to go? Is your meteor a *bolide*, an exploding meteor—does it burst and flare and perhaps separate into pieces?

Also note the trail behind your meteor. After the meteor itself disappears, does it leave a mystically glowing trail for a fraction of a second or for many seconds? This trail is actually the shining of gases which at certain heights in our atmosphere can be "ionized" (have particular electrons in their atoms moved in such a way as to give off energy) by a passing meteor.

It is extremely rare for a meteor to survive its fiery journey and actually reach the ground as a *meteorite*. But if you ever do see an especially bright fireball, try to write down immediately everything you remember about its appearance (especially how many degrees high in the sky it was at beginning, middle, and end of its flight). Then send your information to the nearest planetarium or amateur astronomy club, or to an astronomy magazine (see "For Further Reading" for addresses).

If you simply cannot get miles away from city lights, can you still be a meteor watcher? If there is a lot of light pollution in your sky, your chances of seeing a meteor in any given hour of watching will be small, unless you go out on the peak night of one of the year's best meteor showers—our next project.

2. Meteor Showers. *Observe meteor showers, keeping separate counts of the shower members and meteors coming from elsewhere in the sky.*

A *meteor shower* is an increased number of meteors,

Table 3 Major Annual Meteor Showers

Shower	Maximum	Above One-Quarter Maximum *
1. Quadrantids	Jan. 4	Jan. 4
2. Lyrids	Apr. 22	Apr. 21–23
3. Eta Aquarids	May 5	May 1–10
4. Delta Aquarids	July 29	July 19–Aug. 8
5. Perseids	Aug. 12	Aug. 9–14
6. Orionids	Oct. 21	Oct. 20–25
7. Taurids	Nov. 3	Oct. 20–30
8. Leonids	Nov. 18	Nov. 16–20
9. Geminids	Dec. 14	Dec. 12–15
10. Ursids	Dec. 22	Dec. 21–23

* Period during which shower produces at least one-quarter of its maximum number of meteors per hour
† Approximate number per hour for a well-placed observer with clear, dark skies at time of maximum

all seeming to come from one particular point among the constellations. You won't see them all appear at this spot, but if you extend back the line of the meteor's path beyond the point where it began shining you'll find it takes you to the same source point, called the *radiant.*

Why do the meteors all seem to shoot out from this radiant? The shower meteors are actually entering our atmosphere parallel to each other but appear to come from a radiant simply by a trick of perspective—the same trick which makes parallel railroad rails appear to diverge from a single point in the distance.

Why do we get meteor showers on the same nights every year? Each year a shower occurs on about the same night because Earth then is passing through a meteoroid stream—a band of mostly tiny pieces of rocky dust which has been released by a comet and spread all around the comet's orbit. In other words, the "parent" comet may

Some Visible	Number per Hour †	Time ‡	Direction of Radiant §
Jan. 1–6	40	6:00 A.M.	North
Apr. 18–25	15	12:00 A.M.	High South
Apr. 21–May 12	10	4:00 A.M.	Southeast
July 15–Aug. 29	25	2:00 A.M.	South
July 23–Aug. 20	50	4:00 A.M.	North
Oct. 2–Nov. 7	25	4:00 A.M.	South
Sep. 15–Dec. 15	10	12:00 A.M.	South
Nov. 14–20	5	5:00 A.M.	South
Dec. 4–16	50	2:00 A.M.	High South
Dec. 17–24	10	5:00 A.M.	North

†Time (standard or daylight savings) when radiant is highest around date of maximum
§When at highest viewable for U.S. observers

be somewhere else in its orbit, perhaps not due to return for forty years—or even all used up so that we will never see it again—but we will still encounter its dust and witness meteors on the date we pass near the comet's orbit each year.

Table 3 lists the year's best meteor showers, giving the prime dates and times to look. The names are based on what constellation the radiant is in or star it is near. For example, Perseid means "child of Perseus," Geminid means "child of Gemini," because these showers come from the constellations Perseus and Gemini, and the Delta Aquarids come from near the star Delta Aquarii.

Remember that some years the moon will be in the sky and bright during the peak hours of a shower—so fewer, perhaps far fewer, meteors will be seen. In addition, meteor showers are not completely dependable. Some years there are fewer meteors; other years certain showers may produce enormously greater numbers of meteors. Nor are meteor showers always right on schedule. Sometimes the peak in numbers will occur a day or two early or late—though this can be partly due to our Earth turning not exactly 365 times a year but instead about $365\frac{1}{4}$ times.

You may notice that most showers are at their best after midnight or even just before dawn, so you'll need to set your alarm clock and have a safe place to observe, preferably with a friend or responsible family member. A lawn chair is good to use; depending on the season, warm clothes or bug spray may be a necessity. Even on the night of an excellent display, meteor watching can require a lot of patience. Don't be discouraged if you don't see many (if you live in a big town or city you may see few, and may want to concentrate only on the best one or two showers). Just think how many people have seen only one or maybe no meteors in their whole life—and what a thrill seeing each unique meteor is.

Of course, the primary project for meteor shower observers is to count the number of meteors. You must try to keep separate counts of the *sporadic* (nonshower) *meteors* or the meteors from any other shower that may be going on at the same time. Using a tape recorder may be the best method of doing this, but using a clicker counter purchased at your local supermarket or department store can help, or you can assign people to take turns writing down the totals while the other observers watch the skies. Here's another important point: each person observing should keep a separate tally—don't count a meteor in your total if a friend's shout alerted you to turn your head and you wouldn't have seen the meteor otherwise.

Your meteor counts will bring you great satisfaction. But suppose you want to report your results for scientific use—where should you mail them? Your best bet is probably one of the popular astronomy magazines like *Sky & Telescope* or *Astronomy*.

3. Comets. *Observe a comet with a telescope—and with the naked eye or binoculars, if it is bright enough—and sketch all that you see.*

Comets are the most mysterious class of objects in the solar system and perhaps the most likely to hold clues about how the solar system formed. Comets have been credited with helping supply water and otherwise make life possible on Earth (billions of years ago). They have also been blamed for having almost wiped out life on Earth a number of other times (the most famous example occurred 65 million years ago when most scientists now think it was the impact of a comet or an asteroid which resulted in the destruction of the dinosaurs and perhaps most other species of life on Earth).

Comets can also be the most spectacular of sights in the heavens: there have been occasions in history when comets rivaled the moon in brightness and produced tails which stretched halfway across the sky.

The bad news is that most comets are rather dim objects, usually requiring a telescope to detect and even then only appearing as a hazy patch of light with little or no tail visible. The good news is that when a great comet finally comes along it offers amateur astronomers sights of beauty and grandeur they will recall for the rest of their lives. Seeing even a very dim comet reminds you of how spectacular some comets become and of all the amazing facts and mysteries associated with this entire class of object.

The famous Halley's comet, last seen in amateur telescopes in 1986 and not due back until 2061, is one of the few bright *periodic comets* (comets with orbital periods of less than 200 years). The other comets are all *long-period comets*. As you may know, comets are usually named for their discoverers. The rule is that as many as three of the first independent finders of a new comet get to have their name attached to it (if you're fourth, you're out of luck, and even if you're second or third to chance upon a new comet you must do so before announcement of the discovery by the first observer gets publicized). Amateur astronomers do find comets (there have even been a few comets in our century first spotted with the naked eye). But before you can get serious about trying to become a comet discoverer (including learning how and where to report your finding), you must learn how to use star maps and to observe comets.

And when it comes to observing comets (Figure 6-1), the fact that most are new ones can present a problem: how do you find out about them in time to see them in the weeks or months when they are still bright enough to be visible? Best answers: (1) join your local amateur astronomy club and ask to be notified by more-expert people in your club, (2) read the popular astronomy magazines for news about comets that will be observable, (3) call the Skyline phone message which is updated weekly by *Sky & Telescope* (see "For Further Reading" for details).

Advanced amateur astronomers make careful estimates of the brightness of comets and measurements of their apparent size. But if you are a beginner and get a chance to look for a fairly bright comet and do find it, you should concentrate on studying the appearance and sketching it. Do you see any shape to the fuzzy patch of light which is the comet's head? How concentrated is it towards its center? Do you notice any trace of a tail, and if so, in what direction does it point? If the comet is especially bright or your telescope pretty big, can you detect any color in the comet?

These spinning mountains of strange ice, releasing huge clouds of dust and gas as they pass through our inner solar system, are famous for changing their appearance, sometimes drastically, sometimes in a matter of hours or even minutes. You might be one of the few people watching under clear skies when a comet has a dramatic brightening or other surprising change. So the

Figure 6-1. The bright comet Ikeya-Seki, as
photographed in 1974

lesson is clear: keep watching a comet as many nights as you can, and keep sketching what you see.

THE PLANETS

4. Recognizing the Naked-Eye Planets. *Observe and identify the five brightest planets with your naked eye.*

In order to find out roughly where to look for the planets, refer to Appendices 6 and 7. Remember that there are periods when a planet may be too close to the sun to observe.

If you start learning your bright stars and major constellations, you should have less trouble in identifying the planets. Also, stars are so distant that they appear pretty much as points even when magnified in a telescope and can therefore have their image disturbed by our atmosphere's unsteadiness much more easily than the slightly larger disks of the planets: in other words, stars *twinkle* far more than planets do, and this is a good way to tell them apart.

To help you have a better chance of recognizing a planet when you see it, and distinguish one planet from another, here are some hints:

Except for the moon, *Venus* is the brightest light in the night sky—when it is visible. Venus can never be seen in the west more than a few hours after sunset, or in the east more than a few hours before sunrise.

Jupiter is the second brightest planet and, unlike Venus, can sometimes be observed high in the middle of the night. Its yellow-white color is similar to that of Venus. But Jupiter spends an entire year in the same constellation of the zodiac (Venus zooms from one to another in weeks). In 1994 Jupiter is in Libra, in 1995 in Scorpius, and so on around the zodiac.

Mars sometimes rivals Jupiter in brightness and whenever it is fairly bright is distinctive because of its golden-orange color (no other planet has this color, and only a few very bright stars have a similar hue). Mars does stay relatively faint—dimmer than many of the brightest stars—for months at a time. During these periods, you may have to know your constellations well to detect Mars as the interloper, the trespasser among them.

Saturn is almost always as bright as all but a few stars in the sky. Its somber gold color and steady, untwinkling light may help you identify it. But a bigger help is that Saturn moves so slowly along the zodiac—about two and a half times more slowly than Jupiter—that it stays about two and a half years in a typical constellation of the zodiac. Thus you can rest assured that for a few years starting in 1993, you will find Saturn in or near the constellation Aquarius. Then for a few more years it will creep across the next constellation, Pisces.

Mercury is a very elusive planet because it never sets much more than one and a half hours after the sun, or rises much more than one and a half hours before. Most of the year it follows or trails the sun a lot more closely. A beginner should try to spot Mercury after sunset at its evening showing nearest to the start of spring, and before sunrise at its morning showing nearest to the start of autumn. Appendix 6 lists when these times occur in the years ahead. If you see a fairly bright point of light rather low in the west at dusk or east at dawn around these times, and it is not Venus, it is likely to be Mercury.

5. Retrograde Loop of a "Superior" Planet. *Observe and plot against a map of background stars the retrograde loop of one of the bright superior planets (Mars, Jupiter, or Saturn), or take a series of photographs of one of these loops.*

The *direct motion* of the planets is eastward in relation to the background of distant stars. But for a few months every year or so, a superior planet seems to halt this movement and go backwards with westward or what we call *retrograde motion* as seen against the stars (Figure 6-2). After again halting and resuming direct motion the planet will eventually cross back over its recent path—its apparent path—among the stars, having usually traced out a "retrograde loop." (*Note:* inferior planets can retrograde also, and retrograde "loops" sometimes don't get closed and don't strictly deserve being called loops—but these are complications we will leave aside here.)

What is the cause of the strange retrograde motion? The planet does not really stop its orbital movement and lurch backwards for a while. But for several thousand years sky watchers tried to explain this motion by incredibly elaborate series of circles upon circles in the orbits of the planets. The reason the problem was so difficult is that these early scientists were working under the misconception that what came to be called the Ptolemaic system (named for the second-century scientist Claudius Ptolemy) was correct: they thought that not just the moon but also the sun and planets all circled Earth. It was not until the sixteenth century that the Copernican theory proposed by Nicolaus Copernicus— that we live in a sun-centered system in which Earth and all the planets revolve around the sun—was introduced and slowly began to win acceptance.

The Copernican system explains retrograde motion of planets quite neatly. Figure 6-2 shows why a superior planet appears to halt and go backwards for awhile. The key is that Earth moves faster than these outer planets. Compare what happens when you are in a car which passes a slower vehicle: for a while the other vehicle seems to be drifting backwards as seen against the distant landscape beyond it. Earth is like the faster car, a superior planet the slower. You might even think of this as a race of runners or cars around a circular track, with

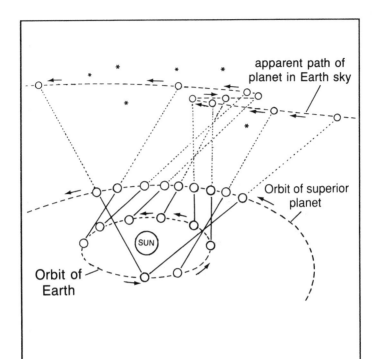

Figure 6-2. Follow the lines of sight from Earth to understand how superior planets can sometimes appear to move with retrograde motion in our sky. (Inferior planets can also appear to do this.)

Earth in one of the inner lanes. Earth has a smaller circle to make around the Sun—and it also travels faster, in order to keep in orbit and not spiral into the Sun, which is closer to Earth than it is to the superior planets and thus exerts a stronger pull.

The explanation of retrograde loops is interesting. But to appreciate retrograde motion fully you should observe it for yourself. Appendix 7 gives the opposition dates of Mars, Jupiter, and Saturn from 1994 to 1999. Opposition is when the planet is opposite the sun in our sky, a rough line of sun–Earth–superior planet occurring in space. The retrograde movement starts a certain amount of time before opposition, and ends a certain amount of time after. The farther out a planet is, the longer a time it retrogrades—but the less distance in the sky it retrogrades. To catch Mars as it starts retrograding you must first observe it, noting its position among the stars, about one and a half months before opposition. Jupiter you must start observing over two months before opposition, Saturn over two and a half months before opposition. At the point in their orbits where they start retrograding, all of these planets are rising rather late in the evening.

How often should you mark the planet's position on your star map? About once every seven to ten days is appropriate. You will have to take into account when the moon is bright or near the planet. When it is, you may have trouble identifying any background stars, especially if you live in a fairly large city (binoculars can help).

Avoidance of a bright moon is even more important if you undertake a potentially far more ambitious project to record a planet's retrograde loop: photography. The basic procedure and equipment is that for photographing constellations and star fields described in Chapter Two. But remember to try to use the same-speed film and the same exposure time each night you shoot the scene, and to photograph the planet and stars fairly high in a sky as dark and clear as you can get it each time. To keep the same stars at almost the same spots in your field of view will make your series of prints more impressive. It will also allow you to produce almost the effect of a movie of the retrograde loop if you shoot slides and then show them in rapid succession with your slide projector. To do a nearly perfect job of photographing a planet going through all of its three-to five-month-long retrograde loop would be a truly masterful accomplishment.

6. Telescopic Observations of the Planets. *Use a telescope to try to see the phases of Venus and Mercury, the rings of Saturn, the surface features of Mars, and the cloud features of Jupiter, Saturn, and Mars.*

Observing details on the planets in a telescope is a challenge. Some nights, Earth's atmosphere above you is unsteady and the planets' images are blurry. But there is another reason why you should observe on many different nights: to build up your experience and train your observing ability. The best way to develop your skill is to practice sketching what you see. Here are some tips about what to look for on the planets.

Venus and Mercury show little or no detail, but they do display phases. The explanation as to why phases occur in inferior planets (closer to the sun than Earth is) was given by Figure 3-6. One of the most interesting times to observe Venus or Mercury is near greatest elongation, when you will see a half-lit phase. Venus is thrilling to see when it gets close to Earth and its globe gets big, but it is lit only along a narrow edge of the Earth-facing side. The long, skinny crescent of Venus when it gets nearly in line with the sun and Earth (nearly at inferior conjunction) is large enough to be spotted with binoculars. (Seeing any phase of tiny, low-in-twilight Mercury is an accomplishment.)

Jupiter is the easiest planet to see detail on. What we see are features in the clouds. On some nights a decent 3-inch (7.6-cm), or even smaller, telescope will show you one or two slightly dark bands running across the middle—the equatorial region—of Jupiter (the dark bands are called "belts," the light bands between them, "zones"). You need only use a magnification of about $45\times$ to make Jupiter look as big in the telescope as the moon does to the naked eye. With a bigger telescope or better (steadier) night, you can see more belts, some hint of details in them and between them, and some traces of different colors. The famous Great Red Spot of Jupiter is normally not very colorful and not very easy to see.

Saturn offers us its spectacular rings, which look continuous but are actually composed of countless separate particles of ice ranging in size from the tiniest specks up to mountain size. The rings are easy to see in virtually any telescope. In fact, they have a breathtaking sharpness and liveness which even the best photos cannot show. Most of the time even a small telescope will reveal a darker outer part, which is the A *ring,* and a brighter, broader inner part, known as the B *ring.* The gap between the two—the *Cassini division*—may even be glimpsed as a thin, dark line in a medium-size telescope when the rings are tilted quite a bit.

But in 1995 and early 1996 the rings will appear so nearly "edge on" (that is, sideways) that they themselves may look like only a thin bright or dark line in your telescope—or not even be visible at all. How can something that spans over 170,000 miles (about 274,000 km) disappear from view? It can because it is only a few hundred yards wide in thickness. A sideways look at a razor blade will cause it to practically disappear from view. The rings of Saturn are tremendously thinner in relation to their breadth than any razor blade—which is all the more reason to take on the challenge of seeing this difficult, marvelous (and changing) sight in 1995 and 1996.

Mars is closer to Earth every other year, and at these oppositions a small telescope may show you a spot of white—one of the polar ice caps—and maybe a dark marking or two on its little orange globe. Only at one of its very near encounters with Earth—for instance, in the years 2001 and 2003—does a very little telescope show much more. (A large telescope and very close approach can reveal literally dozens of details on Mars's surface!)

You will need to gain lots of experience as a planetary observer before you can see details occasionally on Venus and Mercury. Only the utmost expert observers have ever seen any features on Uranus or Neptune (they're too distant, look too small in the telescope), and no telescope on Earth has yet shown Pluto as more than a speck.

7. The Moons of Jupiter and Saturn. *With a telescope, follow the ever-changing patterns formed by the four large Galilean satellites of Jupiter, watching for their eclipses, occultations, and transits. Also, see how many moons of Saturn you can spot.*

You might try this project together with the one about making models of the Jovian (Jupiter's) or Saturnian (Saturn's) satellite system (described in Project 8, "Model of the Solar System").

When Galileo became the first (or maybe one of the first) to see the four biggest moons of Jupiter and realized that they were orbiting around the planet, it was one of his most important discoveries: here was proof that not everything revolved around the Earth, that the Copernican system might be right. We still sometimes call these four moons—Io, Europa, Ganymede, and Callisto—the Galilean satellites.

You can actually glimpse these moons in binoculars when they are farthest to one side or other from the planet (in fact, a few people—myself included—have seen several of these moons with the naked eye under the right conditions). But to see them easily you need at least a small telescope.

If your telescope is small, the moons will appear only as starlike points of light. But you will be endlessly fascinated by their movements around Jupiter. You can see changes in the pattern of them in just a matter of minutes. With a small telescope you may have difficulty in getting good views of them disappearing behind the edge of Jupiter (an occultation), or fading in the shadow of Jupiter (an eclipse), or crossing the face of Jupiter (a transit), or having their shadows cross the face of Jupiter (a shadow transit). But do try to see some of these events. On many nights, all you have to do is look. But if you do want more information about where each moon will be, etc., you can find it every month in the popular astronomy magazines.

What about the moons of Saturn? Saturn is much more distant, but one of its moons—the giant Titan— is fairly easy to see in a small telescope. How many more little "stars"—other moons—you can see near Saturn will depend on the size of your telescope, your sky conditions, and your observing ability. Look for some of the numerous other moons whenever you get a chance.

8. Model of the Solar System. *Make a scale model of the solar system in your neighborhood or your school by following the guidelines of "the Thousand-Yard Model."*

When we move away from our Earth and moon, we begin to encounter distances between worlds that truly boggle the mind. In ten years a very busy driver could run up as much mileage on several cars to have taken him as far as the moon. But even the nearest approach of the nearest planet, Venus, brings that world no closer than about 100 times the moon's distance from us— you'd have to drive a car for a thousand years.

How can we best visualize the incredible distances between the planets? If you have lots and lots of space— a huge field at school or a long, straight street running by your home—you can try making author Guy Ottewell's model of the solar system, variously called "the Thousand-Yard Model" or "the Earth as a Peppercorn" (a peppercorn is very small, especially compared to the 8-inch-wide (20-cm) ball used for the sun in this model).

In Ottewell's model, the average distance to Pluto is just over 1,000 yards (914 m)—over half a mile (0.8 km), too far for most groups to walk out to and back at a school. You can have a few able-bodied people run the models of the outer planets out this far, or point at a landmark you've measured (perhaps with a car odometer) as being that far away. Why must the distances be so great (not unwalkable, but impractical for the time and energy of many folks)? Because, argues Ottewell, make the distances between planets smaller, and the size of the objects representing the planets must be made virtually too small to see.

Table 4 gives the figures for how big the planets should be and how big distances between them should be. On this scale, 1 inch (2.5 cm) equals 100,000 miles (160,000 km). You can be as precise or imprecise as you want to be. For instance, most people who perform this demonstration prefer to simply judge how long their stride is and pace off the distance that way.

Our next project is about making models of the satellite systems of Jupiter and Saturn, and these will be more manageable if you're looking for a science project you can put on a table! Your whole school—and maybe a local newspaper or TV station—can become involved in a demonstration of the Thousand-Yard Model of the solar system.

The most stunning single point in making the model may be when you pace off the distance to Jupiter. The distances between the sun and tiny planets Mercury, Venus, Earth, and Mars will already have amazed everyone. Then you put a chestnut—or other object almost an inch in diameter—that is Jupiter, 135 yards (123 m) away from the 8-inch-wide ball that is the sun. Yes, 135 yards—far more than a football field's length! It sounds astounding. But when you walk it and *see* it for yourself you will be far more astounded. (I've made the model a number of times over the years—and it never ceases to amaze me.)

Table 4 Data for the Thousand-Yard Model

	miles	dimensions for model yards	inches
Diameter of sun	800,000		8 (Ball)
Distance from sun to Mercury	36,000,000	10	
Diameter of Mercury	3,000		.03 (Pinhead)
Distance from orbit of Mercury to Venus	31,000,000	9	
Diameter of Venus	7,500		.08 (Peppercorn)
Distance from orbit of Venus to Earth	26,000,000	7	
Diameter of Earth	8,000		.08 (Peppercorn)
Distance from orbit of Earth to Mars	49,000,000	14	
Diameter of Mars	4,000		.04 (Pinhead)
Distance from orbit of Mars to Jupiter	342,000,000	95	
Diameter of Jupiter	90,000		.9 (Chestnut)
Distance from orbit of Jupiter to Saturn	403,000,000	112	
Diameter of Saturn	75,000		.75 (Filbert)
Distance from orbit of Saturn to Uranus	896,000,000	249	
Diameter of Uranus	32,000		.3 (Peanut)
Distance from orbit of Uranus to Neptune	1,011,000,000	281	
Diameter of Neptune	30,000		.3 (Peanut)
Distance from orbit of Neptune to Pluto	872,000,000	242	
Diameter of Pluto	1,400		.01 (Pinhead)
Total of distances	3,666,000,000	1,019	
Distance from Earth to moon	240,000		2.4
Diameter of moon	2,000		.02 (Pinhead)

Table 5 Data on Jupiter, Saturn, and Their Satellite Systems

Jupiter: (equatorial) diameter 88,700 miles, radius 44,350 miles

	Distance in Miles*	Diameter in Miles
Primary ring (inner edge)	76,300	
Metis	79,500	(25)
Primary ring (outer edge)	80,200	
Adrastea	80,000	(15)
Amalthea	112,000	106
Thebe	138,000	(60)
IO	262,000	2,260
EUROPA	417,000	1,950
GANYMEDE	665,000	3,270
CALLISTO	1,171,000	2,980
Leda	6,698,000	(10)
Himalia	7,127,000	115
Lysithea	7,276,000	(20)
Elara	7,295,000	45
Ananke	13,173,000	(20)
Carme	13,888,000	(25)
Pasiphae	14,497,000	(30)
Sinope	14,521,000	(20)

*As measured from center of planet

(continued on following page)

Table 5 continued

Saturn: (equatorial) diameter 74,600 miles, radius 37,300 miles

	Distance in Miles *	Diameter in Miles
C ring (inner edge)	45,500	
C ring (outer edge)	56,900	
B ring (inner edge)	56,900	
B ring (outer edge)	73,000	
A ring (inner edge)	75,100	
Encke division and unnamed moon	82,900	
A ring (outer edge)	83,600	
Atlas	85,100	20
Prometheus	86,400	60
Pandora	88,200	55
Janus	93,800	120
Epimetheus	93,800	75
MIMAS	116,000	240
ENCELADUS	148,000	310
TETHYS	183,000	660
Telesto	183,000	15
Calypso	183,000	15
DIONE	235,000	695
Helene	235,000	20
RHEA	327,000	950
TITAN	759,000	3,200
HYPERION	920,000	160
IAPETUS	2,213,000	905
Phoebe	8,053,000	135

* As measured from center of planet

116

After doing the Thousand-Yard Model, what more can you do to make people marvel? Ask them to guess how far away the nearest star system would be on this scale. A mile (1.6 km), 10 miles (16 km), 100 miles (160 km)? No, 4,000 miles (6,400 km). That's a thousand miles farther than the distance from Boston to San Diego. If our large field with a ball and a few tiny nuts and pinheads were in New York City we would have to imagine all of North America deserted—except for a similar field in Alaska, containing the three balls of the three-star Alpha Centauri system, and perhaps its own few little bits of planetary rubble, almost too small to see.

(You can get much additional helpful information about making the Thousand-Yard Model by obtaining the pamphlet on it by its inventor Guy Ottewell, Astronomical Workshop, Furman U., Greenville, SC 29613.)

9. Models of the Jupiter and Saturn Systems. *Make a model of Jupiter and its major moons, or Saturn and its major moons.*

The planets' sizes are incredibly smaller than the distances between them. But the giant planets Jupiter and Saturn loom reasonably large in relation to the distance to their most important moons. In Table 5 are found the diameters of these planets and their moons and the separation between each planet and moon. Here is a chance for a highly original science fair project. It is up to you to decide how big you can make Jupiter or Saturn and still have room to show some of the moons without needing too much space on a display table. Which moons are big enough to show at the size they really are in relation to their planets?

Exploring Stars, Clusters, Nebulas, and Galaxies

STARS

1. The Brightest Stars. *Observe the brightest stars of each season, learning what is notable about all of them.*

If you live in a big city, you may have a tough time seeing many stars. But you should fairly easily be able to find all the stars of first magnitude, the first class of brightness. By observing these stars and thinking over some of the facts about them, you will have an excellent idea of the many kinds of stars that exist.

There is so much to say about each of these stars that we can only say a few of the most important things in Table 6. The stars are grouped according to the season when they are best seen in the evening. You can go out later at night and view stars of the next season. If you go out just before dawn, you may see stars as much as two seasons ahead.

2. The Major Constellations. *Find the most important constellations for each season and locate the stars which form the key parts of their outline.*

Seeing the brightest stars is easier than identifying most constellations. Anyone who lives in a large city may only be able to identify the most prominent of the constellations listed with notes in Table 7. But we should all try to observe these official star patterns. After all, these patterns not only are useful for helping us find our way around the heavens, but they are beautiful in themselves—and have helped people remember for thousands of years some of humanity's greatest legends and myths.

The star maps for each season (Figs. 2-1–2-4) will help you find these constellations (remember, as with the brightest stars, that you can see the constellations of the next season if you stay up late enough). You may also wish to refer to Appendix 2 for an alphabetical listing of all the constellations, major and minor, both those visible in our part of the world and those visible to observers who live in more southern lands.

STAR CLUSTERS AND NEBULAS

3. Star Clusters. *Observe with naked eye, binoculars, or telescope as many of the open star clusters and globular star clusters as you can from Table 8, and take notes or make sketches of each one.*

Sometimes a number of stars are born together from a nebula—a cloud of gas and dust in space—and manage to stay together as a glorious group for millions or even billions of years. Such groupings of dozens or hundreds or thousands or even a few million stars in space are called *star clusters*.

There are two radically different types of star clusters, *open* (also called galactic) *clusters* and *globular clusters* (for a definition and description of these two types, see the subsection "Star Clusters" in Chapter Three). You'll notice in Table 8 that almost all the globulars are found in summer skies. This is because they are mighty, distant objects situated in the form of a great halo around the center of our galaxy—a center toward which we look when we gaze at a place in the summer constellation Sagittarius.

Open clusters come in a greater variety than globu-

Table 6 The Brightest Stars Visible from Most of the United States, by Season

WINTER

Star	Constellation	Magnitude	Color
Sirius	Canis Major	−1.46	blue-white
Capella	Auriga	+0.08	yellow
Rigel	Orion	0.12	blue-white
Procyon	Canis Minor	0.38	white
Betelgeuse	Orion	0.50*	deep orange
Aldebaran	Taurus	0.85*	light orange
Pollux	Gemini	1.14	light orange

WINTER

Remarks

"The Dog Star"; gave rise to belief about hot "Dog Days" of summer; closest bright star visible to most of U.S., just 8.6 light-years away; has white dwarf companion; its dawn rising foretold annual Nile flood and marked New Year in important period of ancient Egyptian history.

Name means "she-goat"—mother goat held by Auriga the Charioteer; actually two giant yellow suns (with two dwarf companions).

Classic blue giant star, 55,000 times more luminous than our sun; marks Orion's west knee.

Has even smaller white dwarf companion than Sirius does; at 11.4 light-years only slightly farther than Sirius; some people see a slight yellow tint in it.

Most famous red giant star, and brightest in our sky; possibly biggest star known—may average about 290 times wider than our sun; size, brightness vary; best way to pronounce name may be BET-el-joos.

Bright eye of Taurus the Bull; not actually a part of the V-shaped Hyades star cluster (which is twice as far); name means "the follower" (of the Pleiades).

Brighter of the two brightest Gemini stars. The other, Castor, is a double star in telescopes and is really a six-star system.

(continued on following page)

121

SPRING

Star	Constellation	Magnitude	Color
Arcturus	Boötes	−0.04	orange-yellow
Spica	Virgo	+0.98*	white
Regulus	Leo	1.35	white

SUMMER

Star	Constellation	Magnitude	Color
Vega	Lyra	0.03*	blue-white
Altair	Aquila	0.77	white
Antares	Scorpius	0.96*	deep orange
Deneb	Cygnus	1.25	white

SPRING

Remarks

Only very bright star in our sky that follows a highly tilted orbit around galaxy, so moves through space at great speed relative to our solar system and nearby stars; light used to open a famous Chicago World's Fair.

Marks the ear of wheat being held by Virgo the Virgin; an arc extended from the Big Dipper's handle takes your eye to Arcturus, then onward to Spica.

Marks the heart of Leo the Lion; star nearest to the ecliptic, the midline of the zodiac; name means "little king"; a hint of blue in it?

SUMMER

Remarks

Star at top of the Summer Triangle; passes virtually right overhead as seen from around 40° north latitude, where most of world's people live; our solar system is heading for a spot in sky not far from where Vega now is.

Most southerly star of the Summer Triangle; one of closest of bright stars, just 16.5 light-years away; rotates so rapidly it must be egg-shaped.

Marks the heart of Scorpius the Scorpion; second only to Betelgeuse among red giants in apparent brightness; brightness and size can vary; name means "rival of Mars" (rival in color); has companion star which may appear greenish.

Most northerly star of the Summer Triangle; name means "tail" (of Cygnus the Swan); superluminous star, about 70,000 times brighter than our sun; would rival half-moon in brightness if as close to us as Altair.

(continued on following page)

123

AUTUMN

Star	Constellation	Magnitude	Color
Fomalhaut	Piscis Austrinus	1.16	white

*"Variable" in brightness, but of these stars only Betelgeuse and Antares can vary greatly.

lars, but you can notice some interesting differences even between the globulars. And either sketching or taking notes about what makes each cluster unique is a project not only interesting in itself but valuable for training you to be a more skillful observer. Try the outstanding clusters listed in Table 8.

4. Nebulas. *Observe with naked eye, binoculars or telescope as many of the diffuse nebulas, planetary nebulas, and supernova remnants as you can from Table 9, and take notes on or make sketches of each one.*

A *nebula* is a cloud of gas and dust in space. For a definition and discussion of the different kinds, see the subsection "Nebulas" in Chapter Three.

When you look at *diffuse nebulas,* you are seeing the places in which new stars are being born. When you look at *planetary nebulas,* you are seeing the outward gasp of gas from a star which is starting to die. Nebulas are the beginnings and ends of stars' lives, and the remains of the most spectacular ends are those nebulas called *supernova remnants,* the relics of the universe's most powerful star explosions.

Nebulas are also beautiful, their variety of shapes almost endless. But most of them can hardly be glimpsed without a telescope, even if you live far out in the country, dozens of miles from city lights. The Great Orion Nebula appears to the naked eye as a haziness around one of the stars in the Sword of Orion; the Lagoon Neb-

Remarks

The only first-magnitude star in the traditional autumn constellations; the farthest south of the first-magnitude stars visible from
40° N; name pronounced FOHM-uh-lawt.

ula appears to the naked eye as a softly glowing little
puff of light in the summer Milky Way band. But even
these mighty clouds of star birth really require at least
binoculars to see plainly and a telescope to be seen in
detail and real color. There is probably no sight beyond
our solar system which can rival the Great Orion Nebula (Figure 7-1). With a 6-inch (15-cm) or 8-inch (20-
cm) telescope and a country sky, you could spend a full
hour at a time looking at the great multiple star and
other stars scattered through and in front of it, its intense central region, its delicate streamers and patches,
its whole glowing green fan of radiance. Even in a sky
with a lot of light pollution, even with a small telescope, it's not likely you will be disappointed by this
nebula.

The other nebulas may be a different story. They
will not be spectacular in a suburban sky, and not even
detectable in a city sky. You will have to remind yourself that to appreciate the very real wonders that they
have to offer, you will need to change yourself: your
goal is to become an experienced observer who can with
an almost magical skill find whatever trace there is to
see of the beautiful sights you are searching for.

GALAXIES

5. The Milky Way. *Observe and sketch the different
parts of the Milky Way band, noting how much of it you
can see in various sky conditions.*

Table 7 The Major Constellations Visible
from Most of the United States

WINTER

Orion (the Hunter)	Brightest of all constellations; Belt of three equally bright stars in a row; Orion's brightest stars are famous blue giant Rigel and famous red giant Betelgeuse; binoculars or telescope show well the amazing Great Nebula around a star in the Sword just south of the Belt of Orion.
Taurus (the Bull)	Eye is marked by bright star Aldebaran, which forms prominent V-shape of Bull's face with big, close Hyades star cluster; Taurus also contains the lovely Pleiades star cluster; medium-size amateur telescopes show the Crab Nebula, glowing cloud left from a supernova explosion seen almost a thousand years ago.
Auriga (the Charioteer)	Connected to Taurus with star Beta Aurigae (also called El Nath); contains bright star Capella, three dimmer stars called "the Kids" (baby goats), and several star clusters beautiful in telescopes.
Gemini (the Twins)	Bright stars are Pollux and Castor, fairly similar in brightness and only about 4½° apart; naked-eye fuzzy patch of light is M35, a big cluster impressive in telescopes; contains several naked-eye variable stars.
Canis Minor (the Little Dog)	Bright star is Procyon; few other stars; lore says it is one of Orion's dogs.

Canis Major (the Big Dog)	Contains brightest of all stars, Sirius; other bright stars include Adhara; bright cluster M41 not far south of Sirius (use binoculars or telescope); Orion's other dog.

SPRING

Leo (the Lion)	Lion's heart is marked by bright star Regulus, famous for having conjunctions with moon and planets (and sun); front part is striking pattern called "the Sickle," back part a right triangle; Algieba is fine double star in telescopes.
Cancer (the Crab)	Dim constellation, but belongs to zodiac and has large naked-eye star cluster M44 ("the Beehive," which planets sometimes pass in front of).
Hydra (the Sea Serpent)	Longest constellation west-to-east, has compact noticeable little head and fairly bright and orange heart-star, Alphard.
Virgo (the Virgin)	Giant but mostly dim zodiac constellation, includes bright star Spica, double star Gamma Virginis (also called Porrima), and numerous telescopic galaxies.
Corvus (the Crow)	Compact, noticeable constellation somewhat southwest of Spica; contains bright telescopic Sombrero Galaxy.
Coma Berenices (Berenice's Hair)	Features large, naked-eye (in country) star cluster, and lots of galaxies; named for hair of Queen Berenice of ancient Egypt.
Boötes (the Herdsman)	Dominated by brilliant star Arcturus; kite-shaped; contains several good telescopic double stars; supposed to guard the

(continued on following page)

other constellations from the fierce Ursa Major.

Corona Borealis (the Northern Crown)	Cup-shaped star pattern with fairly bright star Gemma (also called Alphecca); several variable stars of note.

SUMMER

Lyra (the Lyre)	Tiny constellation with brilliant star Vega; passes nearly overhead as seen by much of the world's population; features famous double star Epsilon Lyrae, variable star Beta Lyrae, and the Ring Nebula.
Aquila (the Eagle)	Bright star is Altair (with Vega and Deneb the three stars of the Summer Triangle); fairly bright star to either side of Altair; Eta Aquilae is bright Cepheid variable.
Cygnus (the Swan)	Bright, striking pattern also called "the Northern Cross"; offers bright Deneb, the colorful telescopic double star Albireo, and several elusive but beautiful nebulas; also offers prominent Cygnus star cloud of Milky Way and variable Chi Cygni (sometimes naked-eye).
Scorpius (the Scorpion)	Very bright and striking pattern; heart is marked by bright red-giant star Antares; the sting is two bright side-by-side stars, and near it are two naked-eye star clusters.
Libra (the Scales)	Dim but famous zodiac constellation with widely separated double star Alpha Librae (a star also known as Zubenelgenubi).

Ophiuchus (the Serpent Bearer)	Mostly dim but huge pattern with fairly bright star Rasalhague in head.
Hercules (the legendary strongman)	Figure upside down with head adjacent to that of Ophiuchus—head of Hercules marked by fairly bright and colorful double star Rasalgethi; most important telescopic sight in Hercules is great globular cluster M13, on west side of "Keystone" pattern.
Sagittarius (the archer)	Main part of constellation formed by pattern called "the Teapot," due to its shape; most important are the brilliant Milky Way star clouds, star clusters, and major nebulas (Lagoon, Trifid, and Omega Nebulas) in Sagittarius—in whose direction lies the hidden center of our Milky Way galaxy.
Delphinus (the Dolphin)	One of the small but attractive constellations near the Summer Triangle.
Sagitta (the Arrow)	Another small pattern, within Summer Triangle; nearby, in Vulpecula, is the famous Dumbbell Nebula.

AUTUMN

Pegasus (the legendary winged horse)	Great Square of Pegasus, rather bright and big, useful for locating other patterns; head contains fairly bright star Enif.
Capricornus (half fish, half goat)	Fairly dim but constellation of zodiac; contains widely separated double star Alpha Capricorni (Giedi).
Aquarius (the Water Bearer)	Another fairly dim zodiac constellation, but includes pattern called the Urn (or Water Jar) and several planetary nebulas.

(continued on following page)

Pisces (the [two] Fish)	Very dim zodiac constellation; most prominent parts a pattern (under Great Square of Pegasus) called "the Circlet" and the star Risha.
Piscis Austrinus (the [one] Southern Fish)	Noted only for containing autumn's brightest star, Fomalhaut.
Andromeda (the legendary chained maiden)	Connected to Great Square by star Alpha Andromedae (Alpheratz) and formed in part by two other bright stars, Mirach and Almak; Almak is fine, colorful telescopic double star; most famous object here is M31, the huge naked-eye Great Galaxy in Andromeda.
Aries (the Ram)	Small, mostly dim zodiac constellation but features rather bright, orange star Hamal.
Triangulum (the Triangle)	Small, dim but includes large, bright yet elusive galaxy M33.
Cetus (the Whale)	Really the legendary sea monster which attacked Andromeda and was killed by Perseus; has some bright stars in head and Diphda, star marking tail, but most fascinating object is sometimes naked-eye, long-period variable star Mira.
Perseus (the legendary hero or champion)	Bright constellation shaped somewhat like a *K*; note star cluster near its brightest star (best view in binoculars), naked-eye M34 cluster, and famous Double Cluster (visible to naked eye and glorious in telescopes); most famous star in Perseus is Algol, brightest of eclipsing binaries, marking the severed head of the petrifying monster Medusa, whom Perseus killed.

130

Ursa Major (the Great Bear)	Includes most famous of star patterns, the Big Dipper, which contains telescopic double star Mizar and its naked-eye companion Alcor; also in Ursa Major are beautiful pair of telescopic galaxies, M81 and M82, and near the Ursa Major is M51, the Whirlpool Galaxy.
Ursa Minor (the Little Bear)	Pattern also called the Little Dipper, with famous North Star, Polaris, at handle end or tail tip; most of constellation is dim, but two stars in bowl—"Guardians of the Pole"—are not.
Cassiopeia (the Queen, mother of Andromeda)	Looks like letter *M* of bright stars when high in north on autumn evenings; many pretty telescopic clusters; middle star of M—Gamma—is strange variable which bears watching.
Cepheus (the King, father of Andromeda)	Mostly dim but offers Delta Cephei, the classic Cepheid variable star, and the colorful Mu Cephei (use binoculars).
Draco (the Dragon)	Long, winding pattern with fairly prominent head and several interesting double stars.

Everyone and everything you've ever seen on this Earth and, unless you've ever viewed another galaxy, everything you've ever seen in the sky—everything!—are part of the Milky Way galaxy.

Most stars you see with the naked eye are mere dozens or hundreds of light-years away; a few very luminous stars are several thousand light-years distant. But beyond these stars shines a band of glow which on sum-

Table 8 Star Clusters

WINTER

Star Cluster	Constellation	Type	Remarks
Pleiades	Taurus	Open cluster	The bright Seven Sisters (can you see more than seven with your naked eye?), loveliest of naked-eye clusters.
Hyades	Taurus	Open cluster	Rather bright stars which form a large *V* with Aldebaran (much brighter star which is not a cluster member).
M37	Auriga	Open cluster	Very pretty and rich in the telescope.
M35	Gemini	Open cluster	Large, bright enough to be seen plainly with naked eye in country.
M41	Canis Major	Open cluster	Bright, good in small telescope, just a few degrees south of Sirius.

SPRING

Star Cluster	Constellation	Type	Remarks
M44	Cancer	Open cluster	The Beehive star cluster, known since ancient times as Praesepe, the Manger, to which two stars (Gamma and Delta Cancri) come to eat; easily seen with naked eye in good conditions, very big.
Coma Star	Coma	Open	So spread out as to be best

| Cluster | Berenices | cluster | seen with naked eye in very dark sky or with binoculars. |

Star Cluster	*Constellation*	*Type*	*Remarks*
M13	Hercules	Globular cluster	Just visible with naked eye in country, on west side of the Keystone pattern; a 4- to 6-inch telescope begins to show that the cluster's roundish glow is composed of innumerable individual pinpoints of stars.
M22	Sagittarius	Globular cluster	On very clear summer nights it rivals grandeur of M13, despite being low in the sky for U.S. viewers; located just east of top star of the Teapot.
M11	Scutum	Open cluster	Located in the midst of the naked-eye Scutum Star Cloud, this "Wild Duck Cluster" is splendidly rich in telescopes, fans out from one brightest star.
M6	Scorpius	Open cluster	Telescope shows shape of cluster is like a butterfly; bright enough for naked eye; near Scorpion's sting.
M7	Scorpius	Open cluster	Even brighter, bigger than M6 (which it is nearby); well seen in binoculars.

(continued on following page)

133

Table 8 continued

AUTUMN

Star Cluster	Constellation	Type	Remarks
The Double Cluster	Perseus	Open cluster	Side-by-side very rich star clusters; easy with naked eye in country; splendid, with colorful stars, in telescopes; very distant.
M34	Perseus	Open cluster	Best viewed at low power; naked-eye in country.
Alpha Persei Cluster	Perseus	Open cluster	Binoculars or very low telescope give best view of these stars huddled near bright Alpha Persei (Mirfak).

mer evenings (and winter evenings, but more faintly) arches across the entire sky. This band of glow is produced by the combined light of vast numbers of stars too distant to appear bright enough to see individually with the naked eye. What we are seeing are the more distant stars which are concentrated in the equatorial plane of our pinwheel-shaped galaxy, a plane which we ourselves are located in.

Binoculars and telescopes turn much of the glow of the Milky Way band into individual stars, but you can tell more easily what the limits of the band are by scanning it with the naked eye on a clear, moonless night far from city lights.

If you live in a moderate-size or small city you should be able to see a bright part of the Milky Way band, the Cygnus Star Cloud, just about overhead in the midevening in late summer. Out in the country, the band has a dreamlike grandeur, stands out magnificently, and has much detail you can trace. Notice the small cloud mid-

Table 9 Nebulas

Star Cluster	Constellation	Type	Remarks
Crab Nebula (M1)	Taurus	SNR, or supernova remnant	Cloud from a supernova that shone brighter than Venus almost a thousand years ago; dim but interesting in small telescopes; features Crab Pulsar; located near Zeta Tauri, one of the Bull's horn tips.
Great Orion Nebula (M42)	Orion	Diffuse	Brightest of all nebulas; features multiple star system (four stars in small scopes) called the Trapezium; color (green in M42 becomes fairly obvious in quite small scopes); located in the Sword of Orion.
Trifid Nebula (M20)	Sagittarius	Diffuse	Bright, fair-size telescope shows dark lanes which divide up the nebula; associated star cluster.
Lagoon Nebula (M8)	Sagittarius	Diffuse	Visible to the naked eye, near the Trifid; large, but not as high surface brightness as some other nebulas.
Eagle Nebula (M16) (also called Star-Queen Nebula)	Serpens	Diffuse	Mostly difficult in small telescopes, shows much better on photographs (or with special "nebula filters").

(continued on following page)

Table 9 continued

Omega Nebula (M17) (also called Swan, Horseshoe, and Checkmark Nebula)	Sagittarius	Diffuse	Rather high surface brightness, interesting shape.
Ring Nebula (M57)	Lyra	Planetary	Most famous of planetary nebulas, conveniently located between two stars in the little pattern of Lyra; the Ring's hole is visible in small telescopes.
Dumbbell Nebula (M27)	Vulpecula	Planetary	Most prominent of planetary nebulas, bigger and brighter than Ring Nebula; located a few degrees from little Sagitta the Arrow.
Veil Nebula	Cygnus	SNR, or supernova remnant	Elusive for inexperienced observers, and rather dark skies are necessary to see it in small telescope; actually just part of a larger circle of nebula strands, remnants of a star which exploded tens of thousands of years ago.
North America Nebula	Cygnus	Diffuse	Shaped roughly like North America; visible with naked eye near Deneb in a dark sky, but binoculars or wide-field telescope allows us to trace the shape.

Figure 7-1. The Great Nebula in Orion appears as the brightest of the clouds in which we believe new stars are forming.

way up the south sky, the Scutum Star Cloud. Notice a huge dark split in the band from Cygnus down to near Scutum and beyond. This is dark gas and dust which forms what is called the Rift.

If the summer night is not too hazy, you can behold the widest, most detailed clouds and band of all rather low in the south. You'll find them just above and to the right of the Teapot pattern in the constellation Sagittarius. When we look toward a spot to the right of the Teapot's spout we are gazing toward the center of our galaxy. The mighty ball of stars at the center, like some hugest of all the globular clusters, is hidden by clouds of dark gas and dust which lie between us and there. But the Milky Way glow in this region is star clouds lying in the "spiral arm" farther in toward the center than we are, and they are glorious.

In winter we look at a spiral arm that is farther away from the center than we are, at a much less bright and impressive scene. But try to see if in the country you can detect some of this dimmer band running from Cassiopeia through Perseus, Auriga, and Gemini and then down between the two Dog Stars, Sirius and Procyon.

How does a little moonlight, city light pollution, haze, or unsteady atmosphere (look for wilder twinkling of stars) affect how much of the Milky Way band you can see, and how prominent the bright parts are? Keep careful records of sky conditions along with the drawings you do of the Milky Way band on different nights.

6. Other Galaxies. *Observe with a telescope the galaxies listed in Table 10 and sketch them.*

We can't see our Milky Way galaxy from the outside, but we can stare out across millions of light-years and look at other galaxies—some which we think look like the Milky Way, others which we think look very different. Each one of these galaxies is a system containing astonishingly large numbers of stars, usually many billions.

Only one of the other galaxies visible from the United States can be seen fairly easily with the naked eye. The rest really require you to use a full-fledged telescope (not just binoculars) if you want to see them well.

The three major kinds of galaxy, remember, are spiral, elliptical, and irregular—all names given to them because of their shapes.

The *irregular galaxies* are mostly small, faint ones, and so are not represented in Table 10. If you ever travel to Earth's southern hemisphere, however, you can see two irregular galaxies that look like large and impressive patches of light because they are so close to the Milky Way. These galaxies, the Large Magellanic Cloud (LMC) and the Small Magellanic Cloud (SMC), are satellite galaxies; they actually orbit around the many times larger Milky Way.

The *elliptical galaxies* range in shape from long ellipses or ovals to nearly circular. A few of the most impressive are found in the great Virgo Galaxy Cluster. The main region of this galaxy cluster is sometimes called the Realm of the Galaxies. With a small telescope you can hunt down several dozen of the galaxies near the tail of Leo and head of Virgo on a clear, moonless spring night in the country. The total number of galaxies in this cluster is more than 3,000!

Spiral galaxies all are shaped somewhat like pinwheels (with some notable variations), but not all look like pinwheels to us, because we see them from different angles. A famous galaxy we see almost edge-on (sideways) is the Sombrero Galaxy. It has a dark lane running through its "brim"—a lane of dark gas and dust just like the Rift we see in the Milky Way band on summer nights. There are several galaxies we do see from almost straight above or below, so they do look like pinwheels: M51 in the spring and M33 in the autumn are examples (Figure 7-2). But the most glorious spiral is the one sometimes called the big sister of our Milky Way: M31, the Great Galaxy in Andromeda. At a little

Table 10 Galaxies

SPRING

Galaxy	Constellation	Remarks
M51 (Whirlpool Galaxy)	Canes Venatici	A 6- or 8-inch telescope starts to show the spiral structure and strange companion galaxy.
M81 (really circumpolar)	Ursa Major	Fine, bright spiral galaxy which forms pair with M82.
M82 (really circumpolar)	Ursa Major	Odd galaxy, seen long and skinny (strange mottling visible in large amateur telescopes).
M104 (Sombrero Galaxy)	Corvus	Bright galaxy with prominent central dark streak (dust lane).

AUTUMN

Galaxy	Constellation	Remarks
M31 (Great Andromeda Galaxy)	Andromeda	Easy naked-eye sight in reasonably dark skies—appears as an elongated smudge of light; telescope shows bright central area, two companion galaxies, and (if telescope is big enough) dust lanes and other structures.
M33 (Pinwheel Galaxy)	Triangulum	Bright galaxy, but so big it may require a dark sky and low power to see.
NGC 253	Sculptor	A bright, impressive long spiral but rather low (and in a dim constellation) for U.S. observers.

Figure 7-2. Large galaxies consist of billions of stars. Some show a beautiful spiral structure. Examples are the Whirlpool Galaxy in Canes Venatici (M51), shown above, and the Triangulum Galaxy (M33), shown below. Our own Milky Way Galaxy also has this structure.

more than 2 million light-years away, it is one of our closest neighbors, and since it is also one of the largest galaxies known in the universe, M31 appears as an elongated streak of light easily visible to the naked eye in the country and in binoculars in the suburbs and many cities. M31 is tilted only slightly from edge-on and is thought to be about twice as big as the Milky Way.

Table 10 gives just a few of the brightest galaxies. Locate as many of them as you can and draw sketches of them. The farthest are probably no more than about 50 million light-years away. That's close? Compared to most of the galaxies that astronomers have observed or photographed, yes. There seem to be hundreds of billions of galaxies in the universe, and when we look billions of light-years away, we start seeing the mysterious *quasars*—tiny compared to galaxies and yet often giving off more light and radio energy than a powerful galaxy does. The most distant quasars so far detected seem to be something like 12 billion (12,000,000,000) light-years away. The light from them reaching us tonight left them 12 billion years ago—long before our solar system formed, way back in the early days of the universe.

Epilogue   A Thousand
                             Nights'
                          Adventures

We began this book with a look at all the marvels in the sky that two young amateur astronomers, Sue and Bob, got to see in just one evening. If you have read this book and started doing some of its explorations and investigations, you now know that even all that they saw was just a tiny taste of what astronomy has to offer.

There are so many different sights in the heavens that you can keep finding more for all your lifetime. There is a tremendous variety in astronomy: our universe is incalculably rich with wonders.

Time itself will bring you new visions to behold. One very exciting thing about being an amateur astronomer is that you always have special events in the sky to look forward to throughout the calendar year ahead. Some of these will be replays of events you've seen before, maybe one of the annual meteor showers or a planet at its yearly opposition. But even these "replays" will never be exactly the same, especially since your sky conditions—and maybe your surrounding landscape, and certainly you yourself—will never be exactly the same. But each year a few events in astronomy are so rare that nobody alive has ever seen their like before—an unusual eclipse or conjunction or comet or supernova will occur and make even the most experienced veteran feel like a wonder-filled beginner all over again!

And then there are the unchanging stars. As you now know, some of them really do change, altering their brightness regularly, irregularly—even explosively. But it is true that the stars in their familiar constellations do return almost exactly the same in their proper seasons each year. By doing so they become like dependable old friends, friends you can always count on. (Go out and say hello to Orion again this winter, or Vega this summer!) But once you get binoculars or a telescope there is so much to see even among the unchanging stars that you could never witness all the possible views even in a thousand clear nights.

I hope this book has provided not just the information and projects to get you started on astronomy, but also the bit of inspiration you needed to get out there and start looking. Once you have gotten out there and really seen a few of the wonders that the sky has to offer, I don't think you'll ever stop looking.

The Brightest Stars

Star	Constellation	Apparent Magnitude	Absolute Magnitude *	Distance (in light-years)
Sirius	Canis Major	−1.46	1.4	8.6
Canopus†	Carina	−0.72	−2.5	74
Alpha Centauri†	Centaurus	−0.27	4.1	4.3
Arcturus	Boötes	−0.04	0.2	34
Vega	Lyra	0.03	0.6	25
Capella	Auriga	0.08	0.4	41
Rigel	Orion	0.12	−7.1	910
Procyon	Canis Minor	0.38	2.6	11.4
Achernar†	Eridanus	0.46	−1.3	69
Betelgeuse	Orion	0.50‡	−5.6	540
Beta Centauri†	Centaurus	0.61‡	−4.4	320
Alpha Crucis†	Crux	0.76	−4.6	510
Altair	Aquila	0.77	2.3	16
Aldebaran	Taurus	0.85‡	−0.3	60
Antares	Scorpius	0.96‡	−4.7	440
Spica	Virgo	0.98‡	−3.2	220
Pollux	Gemini	1.14	0.7	40
Fomalhaut	Piscis Austrinus	1.16	2.0	22
Beta Crucis†	Crux	1.25‡	−4.7	460
Deneb	Cygnus	1.25	−7.2	1500
Regulus	Leo	1.35	−0.3	69
Adhara	Canis Major	1.50	−4.8	570
Castor	Gemini	1.57	0.5	49

* Absolute magnitude is the magnitude the star would have if placed at a standard distance of about 32.6 light-years. (Magnitudes for double stars are the combined brightness.)
† Not visible from most (or all) of the United States.
‡ Variable in brightness. (Of these stars, only Betelgeuse and Antares can vary greatly.)

Appendix 2

The Constellations

Andromeda (the Chained Maiden)
Antlia the (Air) Pump *
Apus (the Bird of Paradise) *†
Aquarius the Water Carrier
Aquila the Eagle
Ara the Altar †
Aries the Ram
Auriga the Charioteer
Boötes the Herdsman
Caelum the Chisel *†
Camelopardalis the Giraffe *
Cancer the Crab
Canes Venatici the Hunting Dogs *
Canis Major the Greater Dog
Canis Minor the Lesser Dog
Capricornus the Sea Goat (or Goat-Fish)
Carina the Keel (of the ship *Argo*) *†‡
Cassiopeia (the Queen)
Centaurus the Centaur †
Cepheus (the King)
Cetus the Whale
Chamaeleon the Chameleon *†
Circinus the Pair of Compasses *†

Columba the Dove
Coma Berenices Berenice's Hair
Corona Australis the Southern Crown
Corona Borealis the Northern Crown
Corvus the Crow
Crater the Cup
Crux the (Southern) Cross *†
Cygnus the Swan
Delphinus the Dolphin
Dorado the Goldfish (not Swordfish) *†
Draco the Dragon
Equuleus the Little Horse
Eridanus (the River)
Fornax the Furnace *
Gemini the Twins
Grus the Crane *†
Hercules (the Strongman)
Horologium the Clock *†
Hydra the Water Serpent (female)
Hydrus the Water Serpent (male) *†
Indus the Indian *†
Lacerta the Lizard *
Leo the Lion

146

Leo Minor   the Lesser Lion *
Lepus   the Hare
Libra   the Scales
Lupus   the Wolf†
Lynx   the Lynx *
Lyra   the Lyre
Mensa   the Table (Mountain) *†
Microscopium   the Microscope *
Monoceros   the Unicorn
Musca   the Fly *†
Norma   (the [carpenter's] Square) *†
Octans   the Octant *†
Ophiuchus   the Serpent-Bearer
Orion   the Hunter
Pavo   the Peacock *†
Pegasus   (the Winged Horse)
Perseus   (the Hero)
Phoenix   the Phoenix *†
Pictor   (the Easel of) the Painter
Pisces   the Fishes
Piscis Austrinus   the Southern Fish
Puppis   the Poop (of the ship *Argo*) *‡

Pyxis   the Compass *
Reticulum   the Net (observer's reticle) *†
Sagitta   the Arrow
Sagittarius   the Archer
Scorpius   the Scorpion
Sculptor   the Sculptor (originally the Sculptor's Studio) *
Scutum   the Shield (of John Sobieski, a King of Poland) *
Serpens   the Serpent§
Sextans   the Sextant *
Taurus   the Bull
Telescopium   the Telescope *†
Triangulum   the Triangle
Triangulum Australe   the Southern Triangle *†
Tucana   the Toucan *†
Ursa Major   the Greater Bear
Ursa Minor   the Lesser Bear
Vela   the Sails (of the ship *Argo*) *†‡
Virgo   the Virgin
Volans   the Flying Fish *†
Vulpecula   the Little Fox *

---

* Invented in modern times.
† Not properly visible from 40°N.
‡ The old constellation Argo has in modern times been divided up into the now official constellations Carina, Puppis, and Vela. (One sequence of Greek-letter designations runs through the three, a holdover from the days when the great ship *Argo* was still undivided in the sky.)
§ The constellation Serpens is composed of two parts, Serpens Caput (the Serpent's Head) and Serpens Cauda (the Serpent's Tail), which are separated from each other by Ophiuchus.

Appendix

3

Planetary Sizes and Orbital Data

	Equatorial Diameter in Miles	Average Distance from Sun		Orbital Period
		In AU*	Millions of Miles	
Mercury	3,031	0.387	36.0	87.969 days
Venus	7,521	0.723	67.2	224.701 days
Earth	7,926	1.000	93.0	365.256 days
Mars	4,217	1.524	141.5	686.980 days
Jupiter	88,700	5.203	483.3	11.862 years
Saturn	74,600	9.539	886.2	29.457 years
Uranus	31,800	19.182	1782.0	84.010 years
Neptune	30,800	30.058	2792.4	164.793 years
Pluto	1,457	39.44	3663.8	248.5 years

*An AU, or Astronomical Unit, is the average distance between Earth and sun.

Solar Eclipses

Total and Annular, 1994–1999

Date	Maximum Duration* (minutes, seconds)	Type	Area of Visibility*
1994 May 10	6, 14	Annular	E. Pacific, N. America, Atlantic, N.W. Africa
1994 Nov. 3	4, 24	Total	S. America, S. Atlantic
1995 Apr. 29	6, 38	Annular	Pacific, S. America
1995 Oct. 24	2, 10	Total	Asia, Borneo, Pacific
1997 Mar. 9	2, 50	Total	Siberia
1998 Feb. 26	4, 08	Total	Pacific, N. of South America, Southern Caribbean
1998 Aug. 22	3, 14	Annular	Indonesia, Pacific
1999 Feb. 16	1, 19	Annular	Indian Ocean, Australia
1999 Aug. 11	2, 23	Total	Atlantic, Europe, S.E. and S. Asia

Data derived from Jean Meeus, *Astronomical Tables of the Sun, Moon, and Planets*
*Of the total or annular part of the eclipse
†*Maximum magnitude* here refers not to brightness but to the fraction of the sun's diameter covered by the moon.

Solar Eclipses

PARTIAL, 1993–2003
(all visible from some parts of the United States)

Date	Maximum Magnitude †
1993 May 21	0.74
1993 Nov. 13	0.93
1996 Apr. 17	0.88
1996 Oct. 12	0.76
1997 Sep. 2	0.90
2000 Feb. 5	0.58
2000 July 1	0.48
2000 July 31	0.60
2000 Dec. 25	0.72
(No partial solar eclipses 2001–2003.)	

Lunar Eclipses

Total and Partial Lunar Eclipses, 1994–1999

Date	Type	Time	Mag.	Duration in minutes	Duration of Total in minutes	Direction
1994, May 24†	Partial	11:32 P.M.	0.24	104	—	N
1995, Apr. 15*	Partial	8:19 A.M.	0.11	78	—	S
1996, Apr. 3*	Total	7:11 P.M.	1.38	216	86	S
1996, Sep. 26†	Total	10:55 P.M.	1.24	202	70	N
1997, Mar. 23†	Partial	11:41 P.M.	0.92	202	—	N
1997, Sep. 16	Total	2:47 P.M.	1.19	196	62	S
1999, July 28*	Partial	7:34 A.M.	0.40	142	—	N

The date and time are for the Eastern Time Zone. *Mag.* means "magnitude of eclipse" and in this case refers not to brightness but to the percentage of the moon's diameter covered by the Earth's umbra (central shadow). *Duration* is the amount of time the umbra is on the moon; *Dur. of Tot.* is the amount of time the moon is totally eclipsed (totally covered by umbra). *Dir.* is the direction of the moon from the center of the umbra—either north (N) or south (S) of the umbra center.
* Visible from only part of the United States.
† Visible from either most or all of the United States.

Appendix

6

Best Times to View Venus and Mercury, 1994–1999

Venus *

Greatest Evening Elongation	Greatest Morning Elongation
Aug. 24, 1994	Jan. 13, 1995
Apr. 1, 1996	Aug. 20, 1996
Nov. 6, 1997	Mar. 27, 1998
June 11, 1999	Oct. 30, 1999

Mercury †

Greatest Evening Elongation	Greatest Morning Elongation
Feb. 4, 1994	Mar. 19, 1994
May 30, 1994	July 17, 1994
Sep. 26, 1994	Nov. 6, 1994
Jan. 19, 1995	Mar. 1, 1995
May 12, 1995	June 29, 1995
Sep. 9, 1995	Oct. 20, 1995
Jan. 2, 1996	Feb. 11, 1996
Apr. 23, 1996	June 10, 1996
Aug. 21, 1996	Oct. 3, 1996

Dec. 15, 1996	Jan. 24, 1997
Apr. 6, 1997	May 22, 1997
Aug. 4, 1997	Sep. 16, 1997
Nov. 28, 1997	Jan. 6, 1998
Mar. 20, 1998	May 4, 1998
July 17, 1998	Aug. 31, 1998
Nov. 11, 1998	Dec. 20, 1998
Mar. 3, 1999	Apr. 16, 1999
June 28, 1999	Aug. 14, 1999
Oct. 24, 1999	Dec. 3, 1999

The dates given are those when the planets are at greatest elongation from the sun.

*Venus is best observed: in the west after sunset for about three months before and two months after an evening elongation; in the east before sunrise about two months before and three months after a morning elongation.

†Mercury is best observed: in the west after sunset for about two weeks before and one week after an evening elongation (especially in late winter or early spring); in the east before sunrise for about one week before and two weeks after a morning elongation (especially in late summer or early autumn).

Appendix 7

Best Times to View Mars, Jupiter, and Saturn, 1994–1999

Year	Mars	Jupiter	Saturn
1994	None	Apr. 30	Sep. 1
1995	Feb. 12	June 1	Sep. 14
1996	None	July 4	Sep. 26
1997	Mar. 17	Aug. 9	Oct. 10
1998	None	Sep. 16	Oct. 23
1999	Apr. 24	Oct. 23	Nov. 6

The dates given are those when the planets are at opposition. For a few months before these dates the planet rises in the evening; for a few months after, the planet is in the east or southeast in early evening; from about three to five months after, the planet is in the south or southwest in early evening.

Sources of Equipment

Remember that you should probably first read quite a bit about astronomy and try naked-eye observing before buying a telescope or other astronomy equipment. Also remember that you can take a look at telescopes and other equipment at meetings of your nearest local amateur astronomy club.

One way to find out where the clubs are is to call a planetarium in a big city in your area; another is to contact one of the major astronomy magazines and ask for their annual update of club addresses and phone numbers. Better yet, if you are looking for a store that sells astronomy equipment in your area, those annual updates include addresses and phone numbers of dozens of equipment dealers around the United States. Find one that is within driving distance of you which has a store (some are merely plants and offices) that you can visit and look at equipment in. It's best *not* to buy anything expensive on your first visit to such a store. Instead, try purchasing a book or two about how to select and use a telescope (several very low-cost books of this sort are available at the Edmund Scientific Company store mentioned below).

A good way to survey information on a variety of telescopes and other astronomy stuff being offered by different companies is to scan the dozens of ads in any of the astronomy magazines (*Sky & Telescope, Astronomy,* or *Odyssey*). Of course, the information in ads may not be entirely accurate—an ad is, after all, meant to sell, sell, sell products. You have to compare ads, remember what you've learned in books you've read, look over the product reviews in the astronomy magazines. It's always good to deal with a company that has a money-back, no-questions-asked policy if you wish to return the product within a few weeks.

I'll conclude by mentioning two specific companies which have good reputations, a wide variety of astronomical equipment, and are geared towards dealing with not just advanced amateur astronomers but also beginners. This should not be regarded as a special endorsement of these companies. They are merely two out of the many dealers from which you may get satisfactory service and products.

Edmund Scientific Company. 101 East Gloucester Pike, Barrington, NJ 08007-1380. Telephone: 609-573-6260 (customer service). Edmund offers several catalogs of its technical and science products of all sorts, but has always offered various telescopes, binoculars, eyepieces, other astronomy equipment, and a series of low-cost, valuable booklets on telescope use.

Orion Telescope Center. Toll-free number for information: 800-447-1001 (in California, 800-443-1001). Three stores in northern California. Its catalog is devoted entirely to astronomy products, with helpful essays on basic telescope and observing questions. The company has a very large selection of telescopes, eyepieces, other astronomy stuff.

For Further Reading and Other Resources

GENERAL INTRODUCTIONS

Dickinson, Terence. *Exploring the Night Sky.* Columbia, S.C.: Camden House, 1989.

MacRobert, Alan. *Backyard Astronomy.* Belmont, Mass.: Sky Publishing, 1986.

Mayall, R. Newton, Margaret Mayall, and Jerome Wyckoff. *The Sky Observer's Guide.* New York: Western Publishing, 1985.

Ottewell, Guy. *To Know the Stars.* Greenville, S.C.: Astronomical Workshop, 1989.

Raymo, Chet. *365 Starry Nights.* Englewood Cliffs, N.J.: Prentice-Hall, 1990.

Schaaf, Fred. *Seeing the Sky.* New York: John Wiley & Sons, 1985.

Schaaf, Fred. *Seeing the Solar System.* New York: John Wiley & Sons, 1991.

Zim, H., R. Baker, and M. Chartrand. *Stars.* New York: Western Publishing, 1985.

BOOKS ON BINOCULARS AND TELESCOPES

Berry, Richard. *Build Your Own Telescope.* New York: Macmillan, 1985.

Harrington, Phil. *Touring the Universe through Binoculars.* New York: Wiley, 1990.

HANDBOOKS AND ATLASES

Burnham, Robert, Jr. *Burnham's Celestial Handbook.* 3 vols. New York: Dover, 1979. (Best all-around source for observing information for young astronomers.)

Ridpath, Ian, ed. *Norton's 2000.0 Star Atlas and Reference Handbook.* New York: Halsted Press, 1989. (Has been the most popular star atlas for most of the twentieth century, and deservedly so.)

Dickinson, Terence, Victor Costanzo, and Glenn F. Chaple. *The Edmund Mag 6 Star Atlas.* Barrington, N.J.: Edmund Scientific, 1993.

MAGAZINES, PERIODICALS, ALMANACS, ANNUAL GUIDES

Astronomical Calendar. (This seventy-page atlas-size guide to each year's events in the sky is authored by Guy Ottewell and contains giant monthly star maps, planet charts, dozens of original diagrams, and a literate and imaginative text.) Available from: Astronomical Workshop, Furman University, Greenville, S.C. 29613.

Astronomy. Kalmbach Publishing Co., 21027 Crossroads Circle, P.O. Box 1612, Waukesha, WI 53187.

Odyssey. (Magazine for young people.) Cobblestone Publishing, 2 School St., Peterborough, NH 03458.

Sky and Telescope. P.O. Box 9111, Belmont, MA 02178.

Sky Calendar. (For just six dollars a year you get a two-sided sheet for each month with a basic star map on one side and an information-packed calendar with a sky scene for each day of the month on the other side.) Abrams Planetarium, Michigan State University, East Lansing, MI 48824.

ASTRONOMY NEWS PHONE HOT LINE

Skyline. (617)497-4168. (Recorded phone message, updated weekly, by *Sky & Telescope.* Late-breaking news on comets, novae, and more.)

MAPS, AUDIOVISUAL AIDS, COMPUTER SOFTWARE

Astronomical Society of the Pacific. 300 Ashton Ave., San Francisco, Calif. (Catalog of books, posters, slide sets, software.)

Sky Publishing Corporation. P.O. Box 9111, Belmont, MA 02178. Wide variety of books, globes, planispheres, software.

Index